Encouraging Children to Learn: The Encouragement Process

PRENTICE-HALL PSYCHOLOGY SERIES
A. T. Jersild, Editor

PRENTICE-HALL INTERNATIONAL, INC., *London*
PRENTICE-HALL OF AUSTRALIA, PTY., LTD., *Sydney*
PRENTICE-HALL FRANCE, S. A. R. L., *Paris*
PRENTICE-HALL OF JAPAN, INC., *Tokyo*
PRENTICE-HALL DE MEXICO, S. A., *Mexico City*
PRENTICE-HALL OF CANADA, LTD., *Toronto*

Encouraging Children to Learn: The Encouragement Process

Don Dinkmeyer

CHAIRMAN, PSYCHOLOGY DEPARTMENT
NATIONAL COLLEGE OF EDUCATION
EVANSTON, ILLINOIS

Rudolf Dreikurs

PROFESSOR OF PSYCHIATRY
CHICAGO MEDICAL SCHOOL
VISITING PROFESSOR OF EDUCATION
UNIVERSITY OF OREGON

Prentice-Hall, Inc.
Englewood Cliffs, N.J.
1963

12,427

Second printing ...... September, 1963

Printed in the United States of America
C

Library of Congress Catalog Card No. 63-12528

To Jane and Sadie, Our Wives

Preface

Encouragement is one of the most important aspects of any corrective effort. Its significance was probably first fully recognized in the treatment of neurotic patients. There it became obvious that any maladjustment—the retreat into illness, and the many deficiencies and failures which these patients experienced—was due to their discouragement. It also became apparent that whatever flaw existed in their personality development was due to early discouragement in childhood. This fact became particularly obvious when psychiatrists were called upon to help in the readjustment and correction of childhood deficiencies, failures, and maladjustment. No child would switch to the socially unacceptable side of life if he were not discouraged in his belief that he has a place in the group and can succeed with useful means. This explanation of the psychodynamics of neurosis and of childhood maladjustment is characteristic of the Adlerian approach.

It was only natural that a problem which originally appeared to be a psychiatric responsibility soon was recognized as a problem which all parents and teachers have to face.

The problem of encouragement has ceased to be solely that of psychiatric treatment and has become one of education. When it became obvious that a manual on encouragement was needed so that every teacher in her training might be exposed to a more intensive study of the intricate and complex aspects of encouragement and might develop skills which are needed to encourage children, it was natural that Adlerians would write such a manual, and that they would be psychiatrists and psychologists. One of us, the psychiatrist, brings his clinical experience to the common project, and the other, working in a teacher's training college, confronted with the daily problems of a classroom teacher, brings that practical experience.

The educator will be obliged to accept increasingly the knowledge of psychodynamics which emerged in psychiatric treatment, in psychotherapy; and the psychiatrist and clinician who is concerned with the correction of children's difficulties will have to become familiar with the educational setting, its needs, and possibilities. Our combined efforts present such a perspective of the integration of psychiatry, psychology, and education. The teacher who learns to use psychodynamics for the benefit of her students does not thereby become a physician or psychotherapist. Psychology, and particularly psychologically oriented correctional efforts, will become an integral part of all educational practices. On the other hand, the psychiatrist may eventually discover that his "treatment" is very often not a medical but rather an educational procedure. In other words, the teacher will need more than knowledge of subjects and skills of indoctrination; she will need psychological knowledge and psychological skills. The clinician will have to familiarize himself with educational techniques when he realizes that psychotherapy is primarily a process of learning.

The selected reports on actual classroom situations with children were provided by our students in classes at the University of Oregon and National College of Education. Some were also gathered from experiences consulting with teachers in Northbrook District 27 where Dr. Dinkmeyer works as psychological consultant. We acknowledge the cooperation of these teachers in providing us with opportunities to see encouragement in action.

We can hope that this book will not only give valuable practical help to teachers and parents, but also serve as a stepping stone toward the integration of psychological and educational practices.

Don Dinkmeyer, Ph.D.
Rudolf Dreikurs, M.D.

Table of Contents

Encouraging
Children to Learn:
The Encouragement Process

Introduction

At first glance it may appear strange that a whole book should be written on "encouragement." Hardly any other form of correctional influence is as widely accepted and recommended. Everybody working with children is aware of the great need to encourage them and tries regularly to do so. Many people think, therefore, that the need for encouragement is self-evident and does not require any particular emphasis. But is this true?

Upon closer scrutiny, it becomes apparent that the significance of encouragement is far too little recognized, and the means by which one can encourage are even far less known. The unbiased observer who has a chance to see parents and teachers at work finds out that encouragement is not given where it is most needed and that many sincere people who try to encourage fail miserably because they have a misconception about the process. Frequently unaware of their lack of skill and ability to encourage, they may actually be discouraging.

Why is a technique which has been widely accepted as beneficial and necessary not applied effectively? Most people consider encouragement as a supplementary aspect of their correctional efforts and do not recognize its pivotal significance; nor do they fathom the complexity of the process called encouragement.

1

Why is the skill to encourage essential? And if it is, why are parents and teachers unfamiliar with it? To understand this situation one has to perceive the unique educational predicament in which we find ourselves today, particularly in the United States. Our inability to deal with children is due to our unfamiliarity with methods that are effective in a democratic setting. We have no tradition to guide us. The traditional methods of influencing children come from an autocratic past when reward and punishment were the effective means of influencing and stimulating subordinates and promoting conformity to the demands of authorities like parents and teachers. The democratic evolution is characterized by a process of equalization. A member of a democratic society tends to resist pressure from those who try to assert authority over him.

In other words, pressure from without rarely promotes desirable behavior. One can seldom "make" a child behave, study, apply himself, if he chooses not to do so. Pressure from without has to be replaced by stimulation from within. Reward and punishment do not produce this inner stimulation, or if they do, it is short-lived and requires continuous repetition. This is different from inner stimulation. Once a child moves voluntarily in the right direction as a result of intrinsic motives, the chances are that he will continue to do so without any outside influence.

But why do children move in the wrong direction? Why do they fail to do what they should. Learning the answers to these questions is a prerequisite for the comprehension of the significance of encouragement.

With the weakening of autocratic control at all levels of social functioning in the nation, the community, the school, and the family, every individual gains the right to determine his own direction. This self-determination is fundamental in a democracy. Our children share this right of self-determination and make considerable use of it, frequently to the bewilderment and embarrassment of parents and teachers who discover that they can no longer impose their will. What the child decides to do depends largely on his own concepts, his perception of himself and others, and his methods of finding a place for himself. As long as he is not discouraged in his efforts to integrate himself, he will use socially accepted and constructive means. However, if he loses confidence in his ability to succeed with useful means, he will give up or switch to the useless side of life. This loss of confidence in himself and in his ability is discouragement.

The extent to which discouragement is rampant in our society can be perceived best in the extent of maladjustment and deficiency in children. The misbehavior of children is so commonplace that many people are inclined to assume that such behavior is normal, an assumption which has been fortified by the misinterpretation of developmental psychology. There is hardly a child whose parents do not have difficulty getting him to leave his bed in the morning, to climb into it at night, to eat properly, to put his belongings away, to stop fighting with his siblings, to be on time, and to help around the house. Kvaraceous speaks about the "continuum of norm-violating behavior,"* which ranges from these minor transgressions to the most violent forms of juvenile delinquency. All of these children are discouraged in one way or an other. Consequently, each child needs encouragement like a plant needs water. Without it, his growth is stunted and his potential sapped.

For this reason, the failure among parents and teachers to provide the necessary encouragement is almost tragic. Surely, they want to help, to correct what is wrong. They are sincere in their endeavors, but they do not have the tools to reach their goals. New methods are needed to stimulate and influence children, and few parents and teachers are acquainted with and skilled in the use of these methods. Encouragement is so crucial that the effect of any action is actually determined by the extent to which the child is or is not encouraged. Regardless of how parents or teachers may justify what they do, if their actions are discouraging, they increase the child's malajustment. This fact is far too little known, recognized, and taken into account. Once parents and teachers learn to accept the yardstick of encouragement as basic for all their educational efforts, they will drop many of their customary responses to the child's misbehavior and consider entirely new avenues of influence.

So crucial is the factor of encouragement, that once its significance is recognized, it may actually revolutionize educational procedures in our families and in our schools. For this reason, the

* W. C. Kvaraceous, *Delinquent Behavior* (Washington, D.C.: National Education Association, 1959).

process of encouragement must be carefully and thoroughly ex-
plored and our teachers, in particular, acquainted with the full
scope of this highly powerful corrective technique.

   This book attempts to provide the material for a course or units
on the philosophy and skill of encouragement. It should be part of
the training for prospective teachers and can also serve as source
material for in-service training.

   The process of encouragement is complex. It is not enough that
one wishes to encourage a child. Much needs to be known about
the method and even more about the prerequisites to the achievement of encouragement. The intricacies of the process will be discussed in detail in the various chapters. It may suffice here to point
out that the result of any corrective act depends less on what the
educator does than on how the child perceives and responds to it.
The ability to be sensitive to the child's perception is one of the
premises that are so seldom met. Furthermore, in order to have an
encouraging influence one must sincerely believe in the child's abilities and willingness. Trust in the child is often lacking, especially
where it is most needed, namely, with discouraged and deviant children. Parents and teachers are so frequently defeated in their best
efforts that it seems preposterous to demand faith in the child who
has thwarted them. But without recognizing the good in each child,
one cannot hope to encourage him. This is another hard-to-meet
prerequisite of encouragement. Still another is the educator's confidence in his own ability to influence the child. If the teacher is
discouraged in his efforts, how can he encourage the child through
them? It seems that the child is often better equipped to discourage a well-meaning teacher than the teacher is to overcome the
child's discouragement.

   What can be done about this vicious circle? How can we extricate the discouraged teacher from the further harmful influence
of the discouraged children with whom she is confronted in her
daily work?

   The first need is to help the teacher. Growing defeatism and discouragement are affecting many of our best teachers who are confronted with an increasing proportion of socially and academically
inadequate children. These children defeat all the teacher's best
efforts to improve or correct their deficiencies. The same holds true
for parents. Many mothers who have difficulties with their children

are told that they need help first with their own emotional malad-justment before they can help their children. This is not borne out by our observations. When the mother learns to cope more effec-tively with her child, her feelings of inadequacy disappear, or, if they continue, do not prevent her effectiveness with her children.

If the teacher acquires the knowledge and skill which could increase her ability to cope with her students and to exert effective influences, her self-doubts in her ability are bound to diminish, as will her distrust of children who previously were unreachable and now may be quite accessible to her efforts. In other words, if we can provide with teachers the technical skill to become more effective even with the difficult child, the vicious circle of reciprocal dis-couragement may be broken. This is what this book attempts to do. All educators, teachers, and parents *can* learn how to encourage; doing so, they may find some of the most perplexing and difficult problems in their classrooms to be challenging and rewarding.

The Development
of Personality:
one | Basic Assumptions

When one is concerned with the task of understanding and influencing behavior, one operates on certain assumptions about the nature of man. In this section we shall develop our basic assumptions with full awareness that other psychologists and educators may operate on different premises. A definite stand has to be taken on whether man is active or reactive, led or pushed. Allport deals with this issue well:

> Up to now the "behavioral sciences," including psychology, have not provided us with a picture of man capable of creating or living in a democracy. These sciences in large part have imitated a billiard ball model of physics, now of course outmoded. They have delivered into our hands a psychology of an "empty organism," pushed by drives and molded by environmental circumstances. What is small and partial, what is external and mechanical, what is early, what is peripheral and opportunistic—have received the chief attention of psychological system builders.[1]

Our theory of personality development considers man as basically active and relatively free in the determination of his behavior. Behavior is not merely a result of outside influences or of heredity. Man is both active and responsible. He is not a puppet whose behavior is determined by forces beyond his control.

7

Man is purposive and striving. He engages in activities that are meaningful to him; he makes decisions and organizes.

ALL BEHAVIOR HAS SOCIAL MEANING

We recognize that man is primarily a social being. The characteristics which make him distinctly human are a result of his social interaction with his fellow man in a given group setting. It is only within the group that he can function and fullfill himself. Man is dependent upon group membership for his development.

Man's behavior can best be understood if it is viewed in terms of its social setting. We should not consider either man or his behavior apart from the social situation. What is appropriate for Johnny to do at home may be most inappropriate at school. It is always important to consider the entire field in which the individual is acting.

The significance of behavior lies in its consequences. All behavior has its specific meaning in its social context. We need to see the child in a given situation to understand the meaning of what he is doing. The social context is essential, then, for the understanding of behavior.

Social striving is primary, not secondary. The search for significance and for a place in society are basic objectives of every child and adult. Man really cannot exist without social interdependence. The role each individual plays in society and his responses to social stimuli underlie the development of his personality.

The child, then, should always be recognized not in isolation, but as a socially interactive creature. Conflicts arise from interpersonal clashes and not out of some intrapersonal struggle for control.

Problems arise from conflict with other people. They are not the product of some war that exists within the individual. Thus, if we observe the child in his relationship to others, we can soon begin to understand the reasons for his behavior.

Need structure must be understood in relationship to its social context. Satisfaction of needs occurs in relationship to the group and other individuals.

Social interest is more than a feeling of belonging; it is a key concept in the understanding of behavior.

> The social interest has no fixed objective. Much more truly it can be said to create an attitude to life, a desire to cooperate with others

in some way and to master the situations of life. Social interest is the expression of our capacity for give and take.[2]

Social interest reflects our attitudes toward our fellow man. The individual with sufficient social interest accepts responsibility not only for himself but also to and for the group. Mental health and good adjustment require the growth and development of social interest.

The well-adjusted person has concern for others. Social interest becomes restricted in children through spoiling or neglect. Doing too much or too little for the child tends to result in the child's feeling that he does not have to be concerned about his cooperative relationships. Thus, two seemingly dissimilar actions, spoiling or neglecting, may lead to the development in inferiority feelings and maladjustment.

By the very nature of the biological mechanism, the child enters the world and remains for quite some time an inferior, dependent being. He is struggling to overcome this feeling of inferiority. We constantly observe adults who are attempting to move from an inferior to a superior situation in a social setting.

The major life problems of accepting one's responsibilities in work, sexual role, and social relationships, all involve the development of heightened social interest. When one is unable to solve the tasks of life, adjustment problems arise.

ALL BEHAVIOR IS PURPOSIVE

It is essential to recognize the purposiveness of behavior. Actions and movements of the individual are directed toward specific goals.

Behavior often is more or less inexplainable as long as we do not know or recognize its goal. Frequently we hear teachers and parents say, "I just can't understand why Johnny does that; it doesn't make sense." This really means it does not make sense in terms of adult purposes and goals. However, viewed in terms of Johnny's goals, his action certainly makes sense and, as he sees it, is the only way to achieve his purpose. This is different from assuming that behavior is "caused." Operating teleo-analytically, we find that there are goals that explain actions. They are the psychic stimuli that motivate the individual's behavior.

The psychic life of man is determined by his goal. No human being can think, feel, will, dream, without all these activities being determined, continued, modified, and directed toward an ever present objective.[3]

For real understanding, one needs to see behavior in terms of its purposes. The purposiveness of behavior is our fundamental assumption. It lets us view both behavior and all movements as a means to understand the general purposes of an individual.

The perceptive educator can determine the goals of a child from his present actions and movement. One needs to take advantage of the many opportunities available to understand the individual through observation of this movement. We must come to focus on psychological movement in order to see the reason for behavior.

Although standardized and projective tests of personality are helpful in determining the child's purposes, we place much greater stress on the knowledge available from close observation of the child's daily decisions and movements. The test situation indicates what is probably generally true. Observation permits us to determine what is true in the specific social setting. Each child tells us much about himself if we will only develop and use both the "third ear" and the "third eye."

Knowing the goal of an individual and knowing, also, something of the world, we must understand what the movements and expressions of his life mean, and what their value is as a preparation for his goal.[4]

Thus we should see all behavior as part of a movement toward a goal. In this way the individual child's actions, studied closely, reveal his purposes.

This, then, is in agreement with Allport when he concludes, "Goal striving is the essence of personality."[5]

In this way we choose purposivism over mechanism in the explanation of behavior.

In taking the teleological, or goal-striving, approach to the understanding of behavior, it is recognized that some of the goals have neurotic qualities. They are based on a guiding fiction or mistaken assumptions about life. However, our psychic life is determined by the almost compelling quality of these goals.

Thus, there is a fallacy in assuming a direct causal relationship between the environment and ensuing behavior. We instead adhere to the principle of finalistic causality, indicating that in understanding the individual the goal for the future is more important than the individual's past history.

This approach accepts the freedom of choice of each individual in regard to his goals and direction. He decides and acts.

THE INDIVIDUAL MUST BE VIEWED SUBJECTIVELY

Man can only be understood in terms of his phenomenological field. We are influenced not by the facts but by our particular interpretation of them. It is more important to know how the child feels than to know the concrete details of his act. All behavior makes sense to the individual in terms of the way in which he views the world.

To work effectively in guidance, teaching, counseling, or therapy, one must be cognizant of the child's subjective view, his "private logic." Our senses receive images that are interpreted subjectively. Each individual interprets reality in a slightly different manner. Thus, private logic can be contrasted with common sense. These personalized meanings help us to see the importance of viewing behavior subjectively instead of objectively.

The significance of a past experience depends on the way in which the individual has come to interpret it; this knowledge is vital for understanding and influencing behavior. It is more vital to know how the person uses his abilities than to know what his ability is. Many of our problems related to lack of achievement are confused because we do not recognize the importance of the psychology of use. When one takes the subjective view, he adheres to the establishment of idiographic laws, laws that apply to an individual, instead of to the development of nomothetic laws—laws that will apply in general.

EACH INDIVIDUAL HAS THE CREATIVE POWER TO MAKE BIASED INTERPRETATIONS

The child is more than a receiver of stimuli. He has the creative power to interpret and assign personalized meanings to all that goes on about him.

A perception is never to be compared with a photographic image because something of the peculiar and individual quality of the person who perceives it is inextricably bound up with it.[6]

This gives a new significance to behavior and offers new explanations. It demands more than a stimulus-response perception of behavior. It takes recognition of another intervening variable between the stimulus and the response, and that is the individual's interpretation of all experiences. We can predict better when we understand the individual's style of life and characteristic pattern of behavior, but we need to allow for the individual's creative power to give personalized, individualized interpretations to all occurrences around him.

We perceive only what we want to see. This is called "biased apperception." The uniqueness of the individual is the result of what he perceives and how he chooses to perceive it. This creativity also implies that the individual can make choices. He does more than react. He is more than the result of forces.

An outside observer may interpret and label certain experiences of the child as the result of overprotection, neglect, or cruelty. That is irrelevant. Our need is to know each child's interpretation of the events he experiences. Thus, it is difficult to prescribe the "ideal" discipline or management for the home or classroom. One must consider the fact that the child may not interpret actions of the adults in a predictable manner.

Freedom of choice means that the individual can and does decide for himself. He is not merely at the mercy of drives, nor is he the victim of impulses; nor does heredity or environment force him into a specific direction. He uses both as stimuli for his own interpretations, and these interpretations give significance to the forces which he encounters both in himself and in his environment. It is less important to know what a child is born with, than to know what he does with it afterwards.

This ability to interpret our experiences certainly applies to our interpretation of the world and our opinion of ourselves. We make assumptions about the world on the basis of our personalized experiences. Some of these assumptions are fallacious, but we operate as if they were true. They become guiding lines for our relations with people. In the same manner, the developing concept of self is a product of biased interpretations. However, once these opinions are formed, we tend to live up to them.

The stimuli which the individual receives must move through the process of perception and interpretation in order to produce the creative response. Increasingly, this interpretation becomes dependent on the characteristic pattern of response, or life style. We then act on what appears to be true.

Our interpretations determine our thinking, feeling, and acting. Billy's original experiences in school lead him to think of himself as inferior and inadequate. He then tends to function on this basis in future school experiences unless one is able to develop his courage. In the same manner, other children develop fallacious assumptions and, hence, continually participate in experiences which reinforce their present perception of themselves.

BELONGING IS THE BASIC NEED

One of the fundamental assumptions for understanding behavior in a variety of orientations is the concept of the basic needs. One finds considerable discrepancy in the listing of basic needs. We would certainly not minimize the significance of the basic physical needs. However, the significance of belonging deserves more emphasis than it usually receives.

Man has the desire to belong to someone or something. Many of our social institutions develop on the basis of this need. Even the very young indicate their need for identification and belonging. Man is not self-actualized unless he belongs.

Studies indicate that one of the causes of anxiety is the fear of not belonging. The need to be part of the group and to find one's significance through belonging explains many kinds of behavior.

Generally, the more concerned one is for others, the better adjusted he is as an individual. There is a need to cooperate. The capacity to give and take develops in the framework of interpersonal relations, and this resiliency, developed in a social setting, is an important part of normality.

BEHAVIOR CAN BEST BE UNDERSTOOD
ON A HOLISTIC, DYNAMIC BASIS

Man, here, is viewed as a unified psychobiological organism, in which the total configuration of factors must be considered. Man hence is seen as an indivisible whole. This is in contrast to an atomistic, reductionistic approach. It is neither efficient nor necessary to fragmentize behavior in order to understand it. The whole individual, in all his aspects, reveals himself through his movements.

The individual is not seen as a battleground of psychic forces that are at war with one another. Behavior has interpersonal, not intrapersonal meaning. The conflicts exist between the individual and some of the people in his society. Understanding is lost in psychic economy. Understanding is not facilitated through the development of atomistic systems. Behavior must be seen as interpersonal and interpreted as a whole pattern.

Drives, then, are subordinated to goals, which in turn affect present behavior. Behavior is the movement of an "individual as a whole" asserting himself in his social context. All of his decisions and movements reflect his guiding principles and assumptions. While specific actions may differ when the individual meets new and different situations, they remain consistent with the specific life style.

THE LIFE STYLE IS PATTERNED AND UNIFIED

The child's interactions with his environment, particularly within his family, provide him with experiences that he interprets; in dealing with them he develops a characteristic pattern of responses called his life style. Knowledge of these basic convictions and concepts permits an understanding of the individual as a whole.

The child's evaluation of himself and his place in life gives unity to his personality. All his actions, movements, and attitudes are expressions of his life style.

In the formative years each individual is exposed to social interaction with parents and siblings, who play important roles in his life.

His experiences and his subjective interpretation of them lead to the formation of guiding principles which govern his movements through life. Knowing how the child feels about an experience is more important than knowing the experience objectively.

In the establishment of a specific style of life, the child is continually looking for guiding principles on which he can base his characteristic reaction. Once the style of life has been formed, all situations are viewed in terms of his biased apperception.

The development of the life style has been described as follows:

A child's life plan does not grow out of a certain peculiarity nor out of isolated experiences, but out of the constant repetition of the difficulties, real or imagined, which he encounters. Each individual will find out special ways and means which appear to be serviceable for his special plan. Out of the individual's special life plan develops the life style which characterizes him and everything he does. His thoughts, actions and wishes seize upon definite symbols and conform to definite patterns. The life style is comparable to a characteristic theme in a piece of music. It brings the rhythm of recurrence into our lives. Everyone offers the stoutest opposition to any attempt that is made for whatever reason to change his life style.[7]

The life style determines the child's decisions, even though they may be based on faulty assumptions or mistaken views no longer applicable to his present situation. Frequently we observe people behaving in all situations in what we would consider an inappropriate manner. They seem compelled to view everything from their bias in order to preserve the ideas about life and themselves which they have formed during childhood. This biased apperception which we all develop is our means of justifying any mistaken behavior. Many of the difficulties of life are a result of basic mistaken convictions inherent in our life style. We "create" our experiences according to our preconceived ideas.

This approach recognizes that the individual's behavior is affected by more than just heredity and environment. The self, as evidenced in the life style, plays a major role in behavior. Each individual's subjective psychological field determines his actions and movements. This means that man helps to "make" his own environment. The environment, in this sense, has a greater subjective value than we usually attribute to it.

In the phenomenological approach, attention is placed on the individual's subjective reaction to events occurring about him. His perceptions, even though biased and personalized, determine his behavior more than so-called reality.

All behavior is seen in a social context. Motivation develops for social reasons.

EMOTIONS INTERPRETED IN THE LIGHT OF THESE ASSUMPTIONS

Thus, we can see emotions in a new light. They no longer are mystical driving forces behind behavior. They can be seen as instruments serving the individual's purposes. Emotions have definite goals and direction and are used to support the intentions of the individual.

> The effects are not mysterious phenomena which defy interpretation; they occur wherever they are appropriate to the given style of life and the predetermined behavior pattern of the individual. Their purpose is to modify the situation of the individual in whom they occur, to his benefit.[8]

We create and generate emotions. There is selectivity in the use and choice of emotions, the system, when they are used, and how.

Emotions are social tools and are always useful accessories in the achievement of our goals, be they social or antisocial, constructive or destructive. To understand behavior we must look beyond the surface. If we take emotions only at their surface value we fail to see their purpose. However, we come to recognize that the individual is goal-directed even in his emotions.

Emotions can frequently be used to conquer. They usually enable us to achieve our purposes quite readily. For example, temper tantrums are usually just attempts to attract attention or exert power. Of necessity the tantrum must have an audience to be successful. When it fails to gain recognition and power, we frequently observe considerable reduction in its use.

Emotions can be viewed as expressions or indicators of movement toward or away from people. The disjunctive emotions separate us from people; the conjunctive emotions join us to them. Certainly the individual can use emotions to suit his purpose; therefore, emotions cannot be interpreted mechanistically. Anger, sadness, and disgust are examples of disjunctive emotions. Anger enables the individual to oppose and to dominate, or to hurt and to get even. The person who uses anger believes that he should have his own way; he hopes to achieve victory by such means. Anger which directs itself toward obtaining power is built upon the assumption of inferiority. If the individual were sure of his power, it would not be necessary to demonstrate it.

Sadness, evidenced in exaggerated sorrow, enables the individual to compensate his feelings of inferiority or weakness. Sadness is an effort to improve his position and secure a more effective situation. In exaggerated sorrow the sad individual sets himself in opposition to his fellows. Frequently the sorrowing individual finds his place made easier by the services and support of others. Thus, sadness can enable one to move from a minus to a plus and develop adequacy out of inferiority. The conjunctive affects include joy, sympathy, and modesty.

Empathy is another expression of positive social attitudes. It is the intense identification with one's fellowman. Ability to feel sincere empathy is a sound indicator of social interest and social concern.

To understand properly the purpose and meaning of emotions, one needs to view them in their social context, relating them to purposiveness, creative power, belonging, subjectivity, and the pattern of the life style. Early in life the child learns to use his emotions to his advantage. One trained in observing children can see meaning in these emotional movements. It becomes apparent that emotions are not so much driving forces as they are tools used to serve the child's goals.

A SOCIAL INTERPRETATION
OF THE DEFENSE MECHANISMS

This theory demands a fresh look at the meaning of what we call the defense mechanisms, the methods whereby the individual escapes certain tasks of life. They permit the individual to protect his self-esteem and faulty view of life.

Some of the more common mechanisms and their generally accepted definitions include: rationalization, the giving of a seemingly logical reason instead of the real reason for deficiencies; projection, protecting the self from recognizing its own undesirable intentions by assigning these qualities to others; identification, taking other people's qualities as our own and empathizing with their successes more often than with their failures; repression, the effort to deny our impulses or intentions; compensation, the making up for weakness in one area by excelling in another.

If we look at these mechanisms in the light of the principles of social meaning, purposiveness, belonging, subjectivity, creative power, and style of life, they can be reinterpreted.

These mechanisms serve to assist the self in its quest for a place in society. They are used with a social goal in mind. They are, from the subjective viewpoint, the most effective action at the time of their use. They permit the individual to belong.

Rationalization is geared to making our purposes more acceptable to us. The reasons we give fit in with those that are socially acceptable. They enable us to change defeat into victory.

Projection places the blame on people who are not as acceptable as those with whom we seek status. Projection enables us to belong by placing blame on those outside the group we want to join.

Identification, as a mechanism, is generally made with those held in high esteem by the society. We identify on the basis of the effect it will have on our place in the group. Identifications are always purposive in that they suit the individual's goals. We do not identify with those that would negatively affect our place, from our subjective sense. Identification with those who have little acceptance is generally indicative of a desire to be different and not a part of the group.

Compensation permits the individual who does not do well in one situation to become proficient in something that will give him a place. Through compensation he attempts to belong by performing tasks which make him acceptable.

If we begin by trying to see the purpose in behavior, the defense mechanisms take on an interrelatedness. The individual is directed by the need to belong, to be accepted, to be significant. Each individual subjectively sees this process in terms of his biased apperception.

Footnotes

1 Gordon Allport, *Becoming: Basic Considerations for a Psychology of Personality* (New Haven, Conn.: Yale University Press, 1955), p. 100.

2 Rudolf Dreikurs, *Fundamentals of Adlerian Psychology* (Jamaica, B.W.I.: Knox Publications, 1958), p. 9.

3 Alfred Adler, *Understanding Human Nature* (New York: Fawcett World Library, Premier Books, 1957), p. 29.

4 Adler, *Human Nature,* p. 29.

5 Gordon Allport, *The Nature of Personality* (Reading, Mass.: Addison-Wesley Press, 1950), p. 169.

6 Adler, *Human Nature,* p. 49.

7 Dreikurs, *Fundamentals,* pp. 43-44.

8 Adler, *Human Nature,* p. 209.

The Child's Development

At birth the child enters a society whose rules and limits he has to learn. He comes to a community which has already established certain guideposts and conventions. From the very beginning the child interacts with the people around him. The members of his family are his first society, and he learns to adapt to them. It is from his contacts with them that he eventually reaches certain generalizations about people and how one deals with them. A child arrives at conclusions about effective relationships by observing those around him and accumulating experiences with them. The attitudes and convictions which he is acquiring form the basis for his life style. Knowing the life style is a prerequisite for understanding the individual.

Each child does not merely react; he is an active participant in the solution of problems about him. He is more than the product of hereditary factors and environmental forces; his subjective interpretation of all that goes on both within him and around him gives meaning to his actions. The child can take a stand towards what he experiences; he has the ability to interpret and to draw conclusions. His behavior is based more on the use of certain potentialities than upon the possession of certain traits; in the development of these potentialities, the child's creative power comes into play.

19

To understand the child, one must come to a realization of the fundamental structure of his personality. This basic structure remains constant throughout life. Thus, if we are to deal with the child effectively, awareness of the life style and its development is essential. There must be more than recognition of a variety of surface behavior patterns which appear at first to be unrelated.

> Recognition of the basic concepts governing the formation of the child's personality contributes more to the understanding of a particular child than does an awareness of the incidental behavior pattern which he exhibits while passing through various phases of his development. Every external change which a child undergoes at different ages is simply a variation on the theme, understandable only on the basis of his basic personality.[1]

The careful observer becomes aware that all actions of a child, from infancy on, are purposeful, even though the child is usually not aware of the purposes. We can come to an understanding of the child's purposes by recognizing the goals he pursues. All actions are a part of a general pattern of life, which is based on an evaluation of self and society.

The child quickly learns to turn the attitudes of those about him to his advantage. He soon perceives their responses to whatever he does. If he cries, smiles, or is passive, he evokes different types of attitudes. The child quickly learns which responses he likes best, by which means he can evoke them, in which settings they are obtainable, and with which individuals his methods are successful.

INFLUENCES ON THE EMERGING LIFE STYLE

Family Atmosphere

The parents provide the atmosphere in which the child first experiences social living. His concepts of people and social life arise from relations with his parents. He develops definite attitudes toward the social conventions within his family.

The parents bring to the child the influences of the community. They exemplify human relationships. It is from them that he observes how people deal with each other. Their relationship sets a pattern for all interpersonal relationships in the family.

Families which are competitive stimulate competitiveness in their children; a cooperative family group tends to promote a different pattern for each child. However, the family pattern is not a determinant of the child's behavior. Actually, the family pattern may permit quite opposite behavior in some children.

> Children of the same family do, by and large, show an inclination to similar behavior, developing characteristic values and moral concepts, especially when these are clearly defined and accepted by both parents. We can therefore say that the similarity of character traits in brothers and sisters is an expression of the family atmosphere, while differences in the personalities of siblings reflect the particular position of each child in the so-called family constellation.[2]

Family Constellation

Each child has an essentially different position in the family and as a result perceives all family events uniquely. The child's place among his siblings plays a significant part in the growth of his character. The competition between siblings leads to fundamental personality differences. Frequently as a result of competition, where one succeeds, the other becomes discouraged and gives up; or where one fails, the other moves in. In contrast, alliances between siblings are often expressed in similarity of interests, character traits, and temperament.

Considering the family constellation, one first notices the ordinal positions: eldest, second, middle, youngest, or only child. Each has his own characteristic line of movement, his concepts and attitudes, which will lead to different evaluations of concrete situations and will not necessarily produce the same behavior.

One must be careful to recognize exceptions to the classical statements that have been made about the ordinal positions. A child may succeed in keeping ahead of his challenging siblings, or he may be incapable of carrying out the role of eldest. Absence of a parent may change expectations based purely on ordinal position. Thus, positional psychology considers the psychological response to his position to be of greater significance than the mere ordinal position of each child.

The ordinal positions have been characteristically described as follows:

The eldest child is exposed to a situation where, for a limited period, he is the only child. As an only child it is probable that he receives considerable attention. Then, suddenly, he finds himself dethroned. He must deal with someone who appears to be robbing him of his mother's love. He tries to diminish the disadvantage of being dethroned. He wants to be first, and where he cannot be first he may lose interest. He strives continually to protect his position as the eldest child.

The second child is confronted with a sibling who is always ahead of him. He is not as able as the elder child. He may come to feel that his inferiority is indicated by things that the older can do and he cannot. The second child often acts as if he has extra ground to cover. He has to catch up, to become "more"; more often than not he becomes more of what the eldest is not. He may, for example, become more active or more passive, more independent or more dependent.

The middle child usually has neither the rights of the oldest nor the privileges of the youngest. He has to elbow his way through life. He may feel squeezed out and then tend to feel that life is unfair. Or, the middle child may succeed in pushing both competitors down and thereby gain superiority over both.

The youngest child is the baby. He is the low man in the power structure of the family, but he may well turn this to his advantage. He has a greater chance to be spoiled. He frequently develops characteristics by which he can find a special place for himself, by being the cutest, the most charming, the weakest, the most helpless. Although he may be the most ambitious, it is frequently found that if he cannot surpass all others, he becomes easily discouraged and then gives up in despair.

The only child spends his formative years among persons who are all bigger and more capable. He soon has to develop skills that assure him the attention and help of adults. He may develop charm and intelligence, or he may become helpless or shy.

It is apparent, then, that certain types of behavior are related to the ordinal position of each child. However, positions do not produce mechanical interpretations. The differences in age, sex, special attributes or weaknesses, sickness, and the like, and the way in which parent-child interactions are interpreted are all crucial considerations. For example, the difference in age can mean a different social or economic condition of the family. The appearance of a boy in a family in which all other children are girls may provide special opportunities for the boy. The way in which the children are grouped, on an age or sex basis, can be quite important in the development of character traits. Certainly the difference in age between the child and parents is important. The young parent as contrasted to the middle-aged or elderly parent can affect the significance of these positions in the development of the child. Where the family is large, it is possible for a child to have dual positions.

Personality traits are movements which indicate the response of the child to the variety of factors that influence his position in the family. In considering a child's position we must not only look at what we see objectively, but also give serious consideration to what the child experiences subjectively, his private logic, his biased apperception.

The Life Style

The child, born into a community whose rules he has to learn, is confronted with the tasks of life. He learns how to deal with the people in his primary society. The members of his family are his society, and he must learn to adapt to them. He comes to conclusions about effective relationships in his world. Attitudes are formed which make up the life style. This life style is basic for understanding each individual. The careful observer notes that all actions from earliest infancy are purposeful even though the child may not be aware of the purposes. We come to understand the child's purposes by recognizing the goals he pursues. All of his actions are a result of his general life style which is based on his evaluation of self and society.

The child learns to turn the attitudes of adults to his advantage. He quickly perceives their responses to his crying and to his smiling. The only way the child can assimilate his varied experiences is by integrating them into some system. Through experience he comes to recognize his assets and limitations. The interaction with his parents and siblings assists in the development of his personality. However, the child is never merely the passive object of external influences. Close observation enables one to see that what appears to be reaction is more frequently purposive activity within a definite plan of life. For each human being this plan is distinctive, unique, individualized. This explains why each new situation meets with different responses from different children, depending upon the subjective way in which the situation is interpreted. We need to recognize that all actions are a part of the child's pattern of life.

The life style gives unity to his personality. "The life style is comparable to a characteristic theme in a piece of music."[3]

The life style develops within the child's social field and reveals his interpretation of this environment. The life style eventually enables the child to act effectively in line with his private logic.

> We are forced to regard everything we see and all of our experiences from a biased standpoint, if we wish to preserve intact the mistaken ideas about life and ourselves which we formed as children. The private logic which each evolves appears to justify his mistaken behavior and prevents him from seeing that most of the difficulties and disappointments in his life are the logical consequences of mistakes in his life plan. We "make" our experiences according to our "biased apperception," and can learn by experiences only if no personal bias is involved.[4]

The child's concepts regarding life are flexible during the early years. However, his developing mental powers soon cause him to rely on impressions which coincide with his preconceived ideas. He now adjusts his perceptions to his private logic or personal bias. This biased apperception keeps him from learning from those experiences which do not fit his outlook on life, his life style.

> People make their experiences, not only do they register what fits into their scheme, but very frequently actually provoke the experiences which they anticipate or desire.[5]

The permanent plan, the life style, arises from the plan which the child has found effective in his solution of specific problems. Then, as the child develops, he finds logic to justify his conduct and is unconsciously governed by his life style. Every human being, then, is guided by his life style, which determines his movements and motivates his actions.

The life style provides a behavioral theme; it serves as a unifying principle. Comprehension of the child's life style is the only sound basis for effective guidance in correcting maladjustment.

> Recognition of the basic concepts governing the formation of the child's personality contributes more to the understanding of a particular child than does an awareness of the incidental behavior patterns which he exhibits while passing through various phases of his development.[6]

The child seeks to answer the following questions: "Who am I?" "What am I?" "How strong am I?" "What is my place?" His answers, which are influenced by his experiences in the past and his anticipation of the future, determine the emerging life style.

Certain concepts, such as the self-concept, the self-ideal, the environmental evaluation, and the ethical attitude, are basic to the life style. The self-concept consists of the individual's personal perceptions, the convictions he holds about himself. Any concept that involves the I, such as "I am," "I like," "I do," is part of the self-concept. The self-ideal is made up of the individual's attitudes about what he wants to be. Freud called this the ego ideal, and Rogers refers to it as the ideal self. The environmental evaluation consists of attitudes or convictions about anything that is not the self. Ethical attitudes are the conceptions of what the individual should or should not do. In practice, then, a conflict between a self-concept and a self-ideal could develop inferiority feelings. Conflict between an ethical evaluation and the self-concept is usually interpreted as a guilt feeling. All of these convictions put together form the life style.

As the human being develops, certain basic mistakes emerge. These are flaws in his logic. Some of the more common basic mistakes are:

1. The feeling of inadequacy, such as "I am helpless."

2. The assumption of being something special, be it most unique or most hopeless.

3. Ethical disparagement, such as "I'm no good," "I'm unworthy," "I cannot do what I should."

4. Pessimism about environment, such as, "The world is hostile," "The world is dangerous," "The world owes me a living."

5. Misunderstanding of others, revealed by statements like "You can't trust people," "Unless people do what I want, they are unfair," "People are here to serve me."

In summary, distortion in attitudes about self, environment, methods of operation, and goals can lead a person to arrive at distorted conclusions.

Certainly, each person needs to be understood on the basis of his individual concepts. However, it is interesting to note that some characteristic types of life style are rather frequent in our culture. Some of these types are:

1. I have a place only if I get approval.

2. I have a place if I am in complete control.

3. I have a place if I am intellectually superior and right.

4. I have a place if I am taken care of by others (by a strong man or by a good woman).

5. I have a place if I am morally right or superior (often leading to the next type).

6. I have a place if I am abused and can look down on my tormentors (martyr complex).

The person who depends on approval has perhaps overestimated the importance of winning his parents' approval. Some people may even confuse being approved with being loved. For some, then, being approved is the only way to achieve status. These persons find it difficult to accept criticism; they are overly sensitive; they try to get others to make decisions so that they never have to meet disapproval. They try to please.

The person who has to control tries to manipulate everything. He cannot trust anyone else or depend on others. He needs to be right, and feels that the more correct he is, the better he is. In an exaggerated form this can lead to an obsessive compulsive neurosis.

The person who needs to be good feels that being good alone provides status. He may be perfectionistic and strive for moral superiority. He likes to sit in judgment over others but frequently shows you how good he is by being the first to admit his faults.

The person who needs to defeat others is generally in opposition. He thinks he is entitled to get his way. His major significance lies in his power of rebellion.

The martyr is a person who suffers and collects abuse. His sufferings give him moral superiority.

Social Interest

Social interest is one's feeling of belonging to others and one's concern for the common welfare. Social interest is vital for the social development of the child. It alone permits genuine social participation and interest in others. Cooperation is probably one of the most important skills to teach the child. Frequently one can detect the amount of spoiling a child has been exposed to by noting his disregard for order and the needs of others. "Social interest is the expression of our capacity for give and take."[7]

Character develops in the social setting. The vital factor in character formation is not the environment one is raised in but the attitude one takes toward the environment.

The amount of social interest often determines the success and happiness of the individual's entire life. Social interest is one's feeling of belonging to others and one's concern for the common welfare.

> An individual's social interest can be roughly measured by his ability to cooperate, his willingness to respect the rules of human society, even though their observance may involve personal sacrifice.[8]

It is well to be aware that the feelings which are first directed against the parents or educators frequently extend in a variety of aspects to society in general.

The Methods of Training

We have already referred to the place of the family atmosphere and the family constellation in the development of the personality. Another vital factor is the method of training, for every child experiences different training procedures. Whether they are carefully thought out or incidental and accidental, the child responds to these procedures.

A democratic relationship requires the educator to be firm and kind. Such a relationship reflects respect for both the educator and the child. The most serious mistake to avoid is spoiling, manifested by overprotection, oversolicitude, and indulgence. This deprives the child of experiencing his own strengths and abilities. Training of the child can be effective in many ways in a democratic setting. Simply stated, it must include a respect for order, avoidance of conflict, and encouragement.

The maintenance of order implies a family or group atmosphere which places a value on orderliness. The parent's example may be important, but it is not sufficient. Order can be maintained if each child is clearly aware of what is expected of him and is not exempted for any reason. Consistency is a key to the maintenance of order. Permitting the child to experience natural consequences of his misbehavior can greatly stimulate his respect for order.

For effective training, conflicts need to be avoided; otherwise the child will rebel and prefer to defeat the adults rather than cooperate with them. The parent needs to have time to reflect and observe. Restraint and flexibility can assist in avoiding conflict.

Encouragement is of greatest significance. The child's difficulties are usually caused by some form of discouragement. He will be deficient if he lacks self-confidence. The technique of encouragement is complex, but essential to the development of his courage.

The Goals of Misbehavior

We can assume that the basic aim of each child is to find a place in the group, to belong. The child who misbehaves still believes his actions will gain him significance. He may direct himself toward getting attention, or he may attempt to demonstrate his power. He may seek revenge or display inadequacy in order to get special exemption. Regardless of the goals he adopts, his behavior results from the conviction that this is the most effective way for him to function in the group.

The four goals of misbehavior have been classified as: attention getting, power, revenge, and displaying inadequacy.

The attention-getting mechanism is found in most children early in their lives. The young child is frequently not able to become a part of the group through any useful contributions he can make. Hence, he seeks significance and belonging through receiving, be it love or attention. First, he may seek this attention through socially acceptable means. However, when these means are no longer effective, he will try any method which results in his being noticed. The child would rather be punished than be ignored.

In the struggle for power the child seeks to show that he controls others. He tries to do only what he desires and refuses to be commanded. To do what he is told or desist from doing what is forbidden means to him intolerable defeat. If the adult succeeds in showing more power, the child is only convinced of the value of power and is more determined to win the next time.

Revenge is a result of violent antagonism. Here the child finds his place in the group only by making himself hated. He can no longer hope for attention or even power. His triumph arises out of being vicious and violent.

The child whose goal is inadequacy expects only failure. He uses inability or assumed disability to escape participation.

Footnotes

[1] Rudolf Dreikurs, *The Challenge of Parenthood,* rev. ed. (New York: Duell, Sloan and Pearce, 1958), p. 24.

[2] Rudolf Dreikurs, *Psychology in the Classroom* (New York: Harper & Row, Publishers, 1957), p. 9.

[3] Dreikurs, *Fundamentals,* p. 44.

[4] Dreikurs, *Fundamentals,* p. 45.

[5] Dreikurs, *Challenge,* p. 28.

[6] Dreikurs, *Challenge,* p. 24.

[7] Dreikurs, *Fundamentals,* p. 9.

[8] Dreikurs, *Challenge,* p. 34.

three | *Discouragement*

The term discouragement, which eludes clear definition, connotes both a state or condition and a process. It applies equally to the person who is discouraged and to the process by which he becomes so.

In order to understand the state of discouragement, we need a clear perception of courage, which is also difficult to define. Obviously, discouragement is the absence or restriction of courage. Similarly, the usual concept of courage emphasizes lack or absence of another quality, namely, fear. A person or an act is described as courageous because of the absence of fear and its consequent freedom of action. A courageous person is characterized by acts which a less courageous person would not dare to undertake. Frequently, psychological concepts are not understood in their essence and character, but rather by a process of exclusion. In this sense, discouragement is explained as lack of courage, and courage is assumed to be fearlessness. It is evident that such explanations of vital human qualities are inadequate. They miss essential aspects of these qualities which are crucial for the function of the individual.

31

What Is Courage?

Since discouragement, by its very meaning, implies a lack of courage, we need first to clarify what courage is. In line with the common assumption of lack of fear is the realization that courage implies a quality of perception and movement which is not affected by the dangers involved or by possible detrimental consequences. The courageous person can look at a situation, a task, or an event in terms of possible actions and solutions rather than potential threats and dangers. Therefore, he can move without hesitation, persist without slackening, and proceed without withdrawing.

But, do not such an attitude and procedure indicate recklessness rather than courage—or are the two the same? This question is not easy to answer, because the same quality or mode of movement may appear in an entirely different light to people with opposing attitudes toward it. The economical person is stingy to those who resent his parsimony, and the generous person may appear as spendthrift if one does not benefit from his generosity. In this sense, the timid may seem prudent and the courageous reckless to those who do not see and feel as they do. Do such considerations eliminate an objective basis for distinction? A single act may well elude clear appraisal and proper evaluation. Perceived in the total situation, however, the significance of each act usually is evident. In a pragmatic sense, each act can be judged by its consequences which provide its significance and meaning.

Obviously, the acts of a courageous person will bring about different events than those of a reckless person. Both take chances, but one judiciously, the other without proper evaluation of a given situation. Psychologically speaking, behind the reckless act usually lies a thinly veiled pessimism. The reckless person only appears courageous. Actually, he expects failure and brings it about by his performance which neglects the necessary caution. This is not the case in the performance of a courageous person.

What, then, is the quality, the psychological mechanism, the character ingredient, which produces and underlies courage? Is courage a specific emotion? Or, is it an indefinable innate quality? From our point of view every action expresses an underlying concept or conviction, a cognitive process, which may or may not lead to specific emotions or emotional attributes and manifestations. Interestingly enough, courage is usually less perceived as an emotion than is its counterpart, fear. In reality, both are based on cognitive processes, on basic assumptions about intentions and probabilities, on a "private logic." But fear is obviously of a negative nature, directed against rather than for something, and often against the demands of the situation and its obligations. For this reason, such intentions need strong emotional support and excuses which are easily provided by the apparently uncontrollable emotions involved and displayed. Courage does not need such reinforcement and justification, such frills and trimmings. It can be direct, casual, and objective. It relies on reason and uses all inner resources without waste, deviation, and inner friction.

If one can look behind the diversity of appearance and operational methods, one can recognize the similar thought processes and conceptualizations of both courage and fear. Their only distinction is the sign of direction, one a plus, the other a minus; one for, the other against. Each is based on an evaluation of oneself and the situation, one in a positive, the other in a negative sense. Consequently, one sustains movement ahead, while the other hinders. In other words, courage and fear are based on specific convictions and anticipations.

One cannot say that either courage or fear is based on a single thought or assumption. Rather we find a cluster of mutually supportive ideas behind each. The essential ingredients of courage seem to be confidence in oneself and one's ability to cope either with the particular situation at hand or, even more importantly, with whatever situation may arise. This does not mean confidence in one's ability to solve all problems of life. Such "confidence" is only found in the foolhardy who pretend that there are no dangers, no difficulties, and no defeats and who simply ignore reality and bask in a false glory of successes which exist only in their imagination. It is obvious that we cannot ever hope to solve all of our problems and difficulties, overcome all obstacles and handicaps. What characterizes the courageous person is his conviction that he can work toward *finding* solutions, and, what is most important, that he can cope with any predicament. He is convinced that, as a person of integrity and worth, he can take in his stride whatever may happen. The ability and willingness to accept anything that may come without feeling defeated and without giving up in despair, and the expectation that one will be capable of maintaining one's value and self-respect seem to be the outstanding features of a courageous person.

Psychodynamics of Discouragement

The opposite convictions underlie discouragement. The discouraged person cannot perceive the possibility of winning a battle, of ever solving his problems, of finding solutions, or even of moving toward possible solutions. He has neither confidence in his own ability nor in life; he assumes that he has no chance. He still may try—and many discouraged people try very, very hard, not realizing that in doing so they miss their opportunities or destroy their chances, in line with their pessimistic expectations. The discouraged person is afraid of what will come and sure that it will be not only dangerous, but hard to bear.

Most difficult to tolerate is the assumption of being worthless, inadequate, a failure. Concern with status and prestige and anticipation of losing or at least damaging both are most frequently characteristic of discouragement. This can easily be understood if we realize to what extent the sense of personal value and status concerns us. Humiliation and disgrace, inferiority and deficiency are the most threatening dangers to us all, since we often doubt our own value and do not realize that we have a place in society, within the group in which they operate, being placed there by fate. It seems that our culture is based on moral standards and ethical values which contribute to the discouragement of all, so that it is difficult to be courageous, i.e., to be sure of one's own value, strength and ability, of being good enough as one is. Very few can extricate themselves from the prevalent standards and develop the courage to be imperfect.

It is noteworthy that the assumption of limitations, of inferiority, of inadequacy, as such, does not necessarily imply discouragement. On the contrary, they can and often do stimulate courageous efforts to overcome the deficiency or predicament, be they presented through the environment or through one's own handicaps and shortcomings. The courage to be imperfect, which means the gracious acceptance of one's inevitable imperfections and failures, provides a built-in protection against discouragement. It is this ability to accept what is and to start moving from the given situation, regardless of how difficult, unpleasant, or dangerous it may be, which characterizes the courageous person.

We have to distinguish between inferiority feelings and what we call an inferiority complex. Feelings of inadequacy or inferiority may, and often do, induce improvement and growth, which may lead to success and accomplishment. This is not true of the inferiority complex, which is a deep conviction of one's inability to correct or improve what is wrong. It is identical with what has been described as goal 4 of disturbed behavior in children. The deeply discouraged child tries to impress his parents, teachers, and peers with his total deficiency so that they may leave him alone, expect and demand nothing from him. In this way he hopes that his real or assumed deficiency may not become even more painfully obvious. Discouragement is the final outcome of a process of testing and trying, of groping and hoping; it is the stage that is reached after one has hoped against hope, tried without expectation of success, and finally given up in despair.

Discouragement can be partial or total. One may become discouraged about a particular skill, function, predicament, or task; or one may be utterly discouraged about life, or one's ability to make useful contributions or to achieve. Through a mistaken evaluation of the situation one cannot perceive the chances which exist nor the ways by which improvement is possible. No amount of assurance of his worth, of abilities, and chances for success can move a deeply discouraged person, because he is convinced that his erroneous apperception of himself and the situation is correct. He has the intelligence to find proof for his assumptions; his "private logic" is as convincing to him as any logical process which we develop to fortify any one of our own personal and subjective assumptions. The question is not whether one is right or wrong; more important—no, of sole importance—is what one *believes* himself to be. This alone is the basis for action. Once we have a definite conviction, we create experiences to fortify our convictions, perceive only what accords with our assumptions, and ignore all that would contradict our concepts and beliefs. This is why the process of encouragement is so difficult. If one tries to encourage a discouraged person, one frequently succumbs to his pessimistic assumptions rather than change his convictions.

The Process of Discouragement

All influences which can produce a change in human behavior, be it for better or worse, are, we believe, based on alterations in concepts, beliefs, and, most important of all, expectations. Anticipations and expectations constitute the strongest human motivations. People act in accordance with what they anticipate will happen, whether it is pleasant or unpleasant, good or bad. This is the secret plan which directs all their movements, secret because they are not aware of it. Naturally, what people expect will not always occur, because other forces are at work and may well prevent what one anticipates from happening. But, we ourselves are always moving toward what we expect, whether we like it or dislike it, desire or fear it, although we are usually not aware of the direction of our movement and the intentions of our actions. On the contrary, if our expectation is unpleasant or detrimental, we may, and usually do, deceive ourselves about our intentions. We believe in the sincerity of our hopes, but all the while our movements may be shattering them.

The present state of science, particularly of psychology, psychiatry, and education, contributes little to the enlightenment of our contemporaries. Many experts impress us with our impotence, with the overwhelming forces around and within us to which we succumb as hapless victims. Prevalent concepts of man, of human nature, almost preclude the recognition of the tremendous power and strength which we have in determining our actions, in setting our own goals, and in bringing about our own expectations.

Whoever alters a person's expectations changes his behavior. Some psychologists and psychiatrists have contributed to the general conviction that we are trapped by emotional forces and irrational impulses, by outside stimulations and hereditary conditions; such convictions preclude the realization that our expectations are stronger than all past experiences and predispositions. Regardless of our hereditary endowment of past environmental stimulations, we move in the direction of that which we expect now, from ourselves and from others. Our past experiences are important only to the extent to which they contribute to our current opinions, convictions, beliefs, and expectations. They alone count—but they are also subject to change.

The process of discouragement as well as that of encouragement constitutes changes in the person's concept and expectations of himself. If he is induced to expect more and better deeds from himself, then he is encouraged. Conversely, if his doubt in his abilities is increased, he becomes discouraged. An examination of all the influences which shape a person's belief or doubt in his own strength and ability can clearly indicate the encouraging and discouraging stimulations to which he is exposed. In our time, the scale balances heavily on the negative side. We all discourage one another more than we encourage; we all are much better prepared to discourage.

The Vulnerability of the Human Race

We may well come to realize that reciprocal discouragement was probably never so prevalent as it is today. Our intense social competition permits no one to be sure of his adequacy and his respected place in the community. We have reason to believe, however, that man always doubted his ability to cope with life, to meet successfully the challenges and dangers of human existence. Mankind seems to be susceptible to inferiority feelings which, fortunately, have more often stimulated compensatory efforts than resignation. First, consider man's awareness of his biological inferiority; in comparison with other beings of his size, man is ill equipped by nature to meet its threats. The formation of groups can be considered as man's compensatory solution for individual survival. Intellectual development enabled man to develop artificial weapons as his body was deprived of natural defenses. This intellectual growth exposed mankind to a new set of inferiority feelings. Man became aware of his own smallness in the universe, of his inevitable death and destruction and his limitations in time and space. This cosmic inferiority feeling again impelled compensatory achievements through religion and art. Man strove for eternity, for alliance with a supreme being.

The biological and cosmic feelings of inferiority affected mankind as a whole and, consequently, stimulated the development of the whole human race. A third type of inferiority feeling has quite different implications. Feeling socially inferior to others has meaning only for the individual. Instead of uniting him with others, as do the biological and cosmic inferiority feelings, feelings of social inferiority set him against others. The child experiences his own smallness in contrast to the size, power, and ability of his parents, other adults, and older siblings. Mistaken methods of upbringing often intensify the child's inferiority feelings.

The feeling of social inferiority was probably never so pronounced as today. During the major part of human existence, the individual was firmly imbedded in his society. Primitive man belonged to a collective society. In our civilization for the last eight thousand years society was static, a caste-society in which it was difficult to move up or down freely, regardless of individual abilities or deficiencies. Only when society became mobile through the collapse of feudalism did individual characteristics cause the downfall of an individual or permit him to improve his social status. Nobody could be sure of his place; no matter how high he climbed, he could still fall. In order to mend his own threatened ego, man developed the faculty of discouraging others by looking down upon them.

Competition within the Family

The deadly game of reciprocal discouragement finds fertile ground and unlimited opportunities within the family. At work and at social gatherings, our tendency to look down on others has to be kept at a minimum; otherwise, it would disrupt any work team and make any party or social affair impossible. We have learned to control the free expression of our feelings and ideas so that we can maintain a certain amount of cooperation and surface harmony. This is not true of modern family life, particularly in metropolitan areas. Here no restrictions limit the competitive strife between husband and wife, parents and children, and siblings.

When either parent strongly dominates the family, the full display of competitive struggle may be thwarted. But where the family is imbued with the democratic spirit of equality, each member is for himself, determines his own actions, and usually tries to gain personal ascendency over the others. This does not mean that democracy cannot coexist with harmony and peaceful cooperation. There is no ill in the wake of democracy that cannot be cured by more democracy.

What is most harmful is our lack of training in dealing with others as equals at a time when the democratic evolution has brought a sense of equality and self-determination to every member of our society, regardless of race, creed, color, sex, income—or age.

This last factor is hardly recognized; today our children have won equality and freedom as a consequence of the democratic evolution. It is one of the greatest sources of maladjustment, deficiency, and delinquency among children. The result stems from what may be called the bankruptcy of our educational institutions, home and school, which can cope with children only as long as they are willing to cooperate, to behave, and to apply themselves. If they fail to do so, the reactions of parents and teachers usually increase the conflict. We have no tradition of living with others as equals, and, therefore, are unable to cope effectively with conflicts as they arise.

At the present time, our methods of raising children constitute a sequence of discouraging experiences. We cannot perceive the child as our equal; therefore, we either overprotect or humiliate him. Our families offer few opportunities for children to test their own strength through useful contributions. Adults and older siblings do not let them perform duties and take care of themselves to the full extent of their abilities. Their smallness and incompetence are usually overrated. We suffer today from an often unrecognized prejudice against children. We give them a great deal of freedom without concomitant responsibilities. We let them run wild and then try to revert to autocratic controls, which we do not have the power to maintain in a democratic society. Our children have learned to assert themselves in the face of ineffective parental influences and are usually much better able to influence their parents' actions, while the parents flounder in their attempt to change the children's behavior patterns. Instead of the traditional parental control over children, our children often control and manipulate the parents.

The worst aspects of competition characterize the present relationships among siblings. Each begrudges the others the slightest benefit or advantage; each tries to pull the others down in order to elevate himself. Continuous fights among siblings are so customary that many are inclined to believe they constitute normal and inevitable child behavior. (The fact that this assumption is not true can easily be proved when effective means of counteracting fights among children are applied and the children learn to get along harmoniously with each other.)

The intense competition among siblings in our modern family affects the development of each child. Its detrimental consequences have been little recognized so far. Competition must be distinguished from sibling rivalry. Competition and rivalry may, but do not necessarily, coincide. Rivalry means an open contest for immediate gratification and advantages. Competition is so much more subtle that it has escaped recognition by lay people and child psychologists alike. In competitive strife each child tries to establish his own superiority over the other. Since no realization of equality exists within the family, each child will be considered either superior or inferior to the others. Naturally, no one wants to be inferior; therefore, each has to try for some kind of superiority. Trying to do so, each looks for his main competitor's weak spots which seem to offer him an opportunity to surpass him. Competitors within the family are thus characterized by the development of opposite character traits, abilities, interests, and temperaments. Each child seeks success where another fails, and, in turn, intensifies the other's sense of failure and inadequacy by his success.

The main competition is between the first and second child. As a consequence, the greatest difference in personality traits can frequently be found between the first two children in each family.

The parents, who are usually unaware of the reasons for the differences in their children, reinforce the differences by accentuating the weaknesses and strengths of each child. In doing so, they surrender their influence on the child's development to his siblings. The children's influence over one another's personality development is greater than the parents' who merely confirm the established status of superiority and inferiority between the siblings. This is one of the main sources of discouragement and may well last throughout life. If the child is firmly convinced that he cannot do what his brother can, he will never even try to apply himself in the areas where the other excels. The success of one is usually accomplished at the expense of the other. The good and the poor student complement each other, as do the conformist and the rebel. Even the one who seems to succeed in the competitive struggle usually has his scars, because the less fortunate and unsuccessful sibling exceeded him in some area, however minor or less socially desirable it may be.

Overambition

It is readily understandable that a child may develop the conviction of his unalterable weakness when he is constantly confronted with a successful sibling. One may not realize that his concept of himself is incorrect, because his overt behavior may justify his faulty assumption of being deficient, an assumption which he then successfully conveys to his parents and teachers.

How excellence may prepare for failure is seldom recognized. Most good students with high moral and social standards are exceedingly vulnerable. They are not "good" merely for the sake of goodness; they do not study merely in order to learn. Too many do so only because they want to be better. However, if they encounter a situation where they cannot excel, their whole scheme of movement collapses, and they may give up altogether. Many children who cannot be best in the accepted social way "switch to the useless side" (Adler) and find their gratification in being the worst. Many of our underachievers are actually overambitious; they may have stopped trying, since their efforts were no longer bringing them status and prestige. What other reason is there for trying, for studying and cooperating? Many so-called juvenile delinquents are discouraged, overambitious youngsters who satisfy themselves by violating the law and defying adults.

The push to be better begins in the family and continues in the community at large. Parents and teachers reinforce this tendency, particularly in the middle- and upper-middle-class communities. Many a child who is not particularly proficient or effective is made to believe that he is not good enough as he is. Even the best student is expected to be better, in some area, either socially or athletically; and the one who is good in everything is often told that he should not try so hard to be good *all* the time. Few children find full approval for what they are; but they, too, may not be satisfied because they may believe they ought to be better. As long as the present trend to stir up efforts and achievement for the sake of glory continues, often by means of threats of humiliation, discouragement among our children will be rampant, in the good as well as in the bad—perhaps even more in the good, who can never be sure of their excellence. Children who give up trying may seem to be satisfied with the low level of functioning and achieving on which they have settled; but behind their ostensible indifference lies a deep discouragement which they are too proud to reveal.

The Effects of Discouragement

It is uncontestable that discouragement is a basic factor in all deviations, deficiencies, and failures, with the exception of brain damage and mental deficiency. No one fails, with all the consequent suffering and deprivation, unless he has first lost confidence in his ability to succeed with socially accepted means. Wrongdoing takes so much persistence, endurance, and self-sacrifice that no one would choose it unless he felt he had no alternative. However, there is one great lure in maladjustment and deviation. It is easy to get special glory, attention and power through doing wrong. To excel socially, academically, or athletically requires tremendous effort, industry, and considerable native ability; for every one who succeeds, literally thousands see no such chance. But they, too, can be something special, be admired by peers, feel important, and gain status, merely by defeating the adults and violating their commands. The switch to socially unacceptable behavior is the most frequent consequence of discouragement.

However, it takes considerable courage to continue battling, even in a wrong way. This explains why many juvenile offenders are among our brightest and most capable youngsters; they refuse to give up and continue to assert themselves. Youngsters who are totally discouraged cannot do that. The most immediate consequence of discouragement is withdrawal from the area where defeat is considered as inevitable. No defeat will stop a child's efforts as long as he considers it as only temporary and sees hope for eventual success. In this sense, failure and defeat may sometimes stimulate special efforts and actually cause spectacular successes. But when hope of success is given up, the full force of discouragement comes into play. When a child will reach the conclusion that it is hopeless to try cannot be predicted, but the consequences become evident immediately. And it is often the misguided corrective efforts of a parent or teacher which convince a child of the hopelessness of his efforts. He may seek success in other areas, or, more often, strive for attention, power, and status in new and unacceptable fields of endeavor. But the crucial fact is that he has abandoned efforts in certain areas, which may remain weak spots for the rest of his life.

This is an important fact; most educators overlook the remaining areas of discouragement if a child succeeds in finding areas of special achievement. They usually assume that his talents are limited to these fields and do not realize that preference for certain activities is often the consequence of discouragement in others.

This fact is of extreme significance. Until we learn to recognize discouragement as soon as it occurs, and develop skills to help the child overcome it, we will raise children who are more or less demoralized, regardless of the achievements they may have to their credit. The moment discouragement sets in, the personality becomes warped. Regardless of how limited the area of discouragement may be, it affects a person's self-evaluation, diminishes his self-respect, renders him vulnerable, and makes him timid and fearful. There is always some area, some task which causes anxiety. We need courage to meet the tasks of life and to fulfill our potentials. Any area of discouragement saps a person's courage and strength. He may successfully avoid this area, act as if it did not exist, but he will not be free to do his best, confident of his ability to cope with whatever may come. Discouragement undermines self-respect and integrity. It leads to deviations and pretenses, to anxiety and fear. What is worse, it is contagious.

The discouraged person, sure of his convictions, however erroneous they may be, is well-equipped to discourage the efforts of those who try to encourage him, to correct his mistaken self-image. The process of reciprocal discouragement makes all of us only too ready to give up when obstacles do not immediately give way to our efforts. This holds particularly true for our educators who are inclined to be easily discouraged about children's deficiencies, partly because children are quite capable of convincing them of their inadequacies.

To make matters worse, adults do not know the methods and skills, which are effective in a democratic setting, to correct deficiencies in children and to stimulate them to efforts and accomplishments that they are on the verge of giving up. As a consequence, the essential ability to encourage a discouraged child is a rare skill, practiced only by those who acquired it usually because of their determination not to become discouraged themselves.

The Principles
of Encouragement

four

The child's motivations, the purposes of his behavior, must be made evident if one is to correct his academic, behavioral, or social failings.

Many psychological and psychiatric techniques can be applied to the understanding of motivation. We shall concern ourselves primarily with those techniques that teachers and counselors can use without intensive training and constant professional supervision.

Observation of behavior can be an extremely profitable technique if a frame of reference and a set of principles are chosen that make observation dynamically meaningful. Usually, observation is used for descriptive rather than diagnostic purposes. It can provide vital information if the observer:

1. Knows the subjective field in which the behavior takes place. This requires seeing the situation through the eyes of the child rather than in terms just of the educator's values and experiences.

2. Knows what to look for. Instead of observing what the child does and how he does it, one must see his purposes, the goals of his actions.

3. Records and observes all pertinent behavior, characteristic and routine as well as unusual, since every movement of the child has meaning.

45

4. Recognizes that behavior is not merely a response to outside stimulation, but a creative act of the child in trying to find a place for himself.

5. Is aware of a teleo-analytic frame of reference in the interpretation of the observed behavior.

6. Looks for recurring patterns.

7. Is aware of the child's stage of development.

The essentials of observation then would include knowing the context of the incident, seeing the subjective meaning of the incident, observing in a variety of settings both characteristic and unusual behavior, looking for recurring patterns, and seeing all as movement toward specific goals which the child has set for himself.

To obtain the greatest value in all observation, one needs to be aware of the meaning of behavior. *"To understand a child properly, one must realize that his every act is purposive and expresses his attitudes, his goals, and his expectations."*[1] For those who can accept this orientation, behavior has meaning and is not merely random. Personality becomes unified when the characteristic themes of all of the child's actions are noted. To one who observes mere fragmentary bits of behavior, incidents appear unrelated, and an understanding of behavior is never achieved.

Careful observation, within the bounds of the above suggestions, provides insight and permits fruitful action. One can then note the variety of purposes which motivate children. Some function as though the only possible goal in life was to be first. They either are the best or the worst. Others operate on the assumption that they cannot be liked and that, therefore, their role in the group is to be a nuisance. Some children function only with the support of teacher or mother; others derive their security from the specific role of princess, bully, weakling, or tyrant.

The perceptive observer will learn that attitudes are recognizable not only through observation of the child's actions but also of his posture, approach, facial expressions, and even avoidance of situations.

The trained observer is able to detect purposes and goals. Mere description of behavior has little value except if it is used as a basis for the understanding of purposes.

In order to develop skills in observation one might make accurate notes of anecdotes as they occur. This can serve to discipline the educator in the accurate reporting of essential facts. The material may not always explain the behavior at a particular moment, but it may serve for later interpretation.

Daniel Prescott has presented a valuable description of the characteristics of a good anecdote:

1. It gives the date, the place, and the situation in which the action occurred. We call this the setting.

2. It describes the action of the child, the reactions of the other people involved, and the response of the child to these reactions.

3. It quotes what is said to the child and by the child during the action.

4. It supplies "mood cues"—postures, gestures, voice qualities, and facial expressions that give cues to how the child felt. It does not provide interpretations of his feelings, but only the cues by which a reader may judge what they were.

5. The description is extensive enough to cover the episode. The action or conversation is not left incomplete and unfinished but is followed through to the point where a little vignette of a behavioral moment in the life of the child is supplied.[2]

This provides a solid basis for recording. It also gives a useful framework within which the observer can operate.

The adult needs always to be cognizant of the interaction occurring between him and the child. The child's behavior is always the logical result of his perception of the situation. Frequently the adult's behavior may be responsible for the child's action. Unfortunately, the child's action more often brings about the adult's reaction. Thus, the adult serves in the role of follower instead of leader.

There are a number of ways in which the child's motives may be brought to the surface for investigation. If one is aware of the structure upon which behavior is built, the child's actions take on greater meaning.

The Philosophy of Encouragement

In any attempt to initiate learning or development, the role of encouragement must be recognized.

One of the problems involved in initiation of performance is that of overcoming inertia. This is a difficult enough task in its own right, but it is enormously and unnecessarily worsened if the student

is permitted to be overwhelmed by exposure, without modifying pre-
cautions, to the full scope of the task expected of him. Just as a child
can sometimes be induced to eat when presented with a small portion
of food, after refusing to start on a larger portion, so a student can
more often be stimulated to work by a reasonable partial assignment
than by assignment of the whole task all at once.[3]

We cannot expect progress unless we are ready to recognize that
in addition to the child's assets and liabilities he needs the assistance
of encouragement.

All children need to feel worth while (many call this feeling
"secure"). Edith Neisser lists six attitudes through which we can
give "security" to children:

1. You are the kind who can do it.
2. It's all right to try. Failure is no crime.
3. Provide plenty of opportunities for successful achievement.
Don't set standards so high children are constantly falling short.
4. Be pleased with a reasonably good attempt. Show confidence
in their ability to become competent.
5. Accept children as they are. Like him as he is so he can like
himself.
6. Guarantee certain rights and privileges.[4]

These are some of the very attitudes which can facilitate learning through encouragement. They let the child know you have
faith in him—faith, incidentally, *as he is,* not as he could be. These
attitudes provide more opportunity for success than failure in the
eyes of both the child and the teacher.

An oft quoted educational experiment provides an example of
the effects of encouragement. In the public schools of Winnetka,
Illinois, it was found that children who were not taught to read for
a year and a half after entering first grade managed to catch up
with and even surpass students who began the reading process
considerably earlier. In this experiment, twenty-five children, who
were matched on the basis of mental age, chronological age, and
similar home environments upon entering first grade, were not
introduced to formal instruction for a year and a half. They were
exposed informally to books in the room and were read to. The
experiment went on for seven years. In the middle of the second
grade, the experimental group was behind. By the end of the

fourth year they were a half grade ahead. Their rate of progress went up slightly from then until the seventh grade. Both psychologists and teachers who rated the experimental group and the control group without knowing which was which found that the experimental group excelled in spontaneity, eagerness to learn, and cooperation.

Children in the experimental group never suffered from a sense of defeat at not being able to read. However, in the conventional class those children who for one reason or another refused to learn to read probably felt defeated, and this discouragement could have contributed considerably to the lowered class average.[5] Another reason for the success of the experimental group was perhaps the elimination of nonreading as a means of getting special attention and service or of defeating demanding adults; there are frequently "emotional predispositions to reading difficulties."[6]

Here we see the results of a longitudinal approach designed to test the effects of postponed formal instruction, but also most effectively portraying the benefits of the elements of encouragement. Children whose learning was not impeded by pressure, by rebellion, or by a sense of failure achieved significantly more. Their feelings of self-respect were enhanced.

Training the child necessitates serious attention to the act of encouragement. Bakwin states the need as follows:

> Proper child rearing requires a nice balance between encouragement for self-expression and freedom on the one hand and training for conformity on the other.[7]

This puts an emphasis on encouragement as a fundamental requirement, while recognizing the demands of society as well. We need to encourage in a direction that is not only personally satisfying but socially desirable.

The need for encouragement has been stated as follows:

> At present, children are exposed to a sequence of discouraging experiences. Deliberate encouragement is essential to counteract them. The child misbehaves only if he is discouraged and does not believe in his ability to succeed with useful means. Encouragement implies your faith in the child. It communicates to him your belief in his strength and ability, not in his "potentiality." Unless you have faith in him *as he is,* you cannot encourage him.[8]

The goal of encouragement is to enable the child to develop courage, responsibility, and industry. He needs encouragement to develop his social interest and his willingness and ability to make his contributions to the group.

The Methods of Encouragement

Specifically, the person who encourages:

1. Places value on the child as he is.
2. Shows a faith in the child that enables the child to have faith in himself.
3. Has faith in the child's ability; wins the child's confidence while building his self-respect.
4. Recognizes a job "well done." Gives recognition for *effort*.
5. Utilizes the group to facilitate and enhance the development of the child.
6. Integrates the group so that the child can be sure of his place in it.
7. Assists in the development of skills sequentially and psychologically paced to permit success.
8. Recognizes and focuses on strengths and assets.
9. Utilizes the interests of the child to energize instruction.

Valuing the Child

Daniel Prescott gives us a succinct exposition regarding this method:

> The first factor in a security-giving relationship is a sincere valuing of the child by the teacher. This does not mean forming a sentimental attachment to the child or attempting to make up for his hard life situation by doing special things for and with him. It means having inner conviction that the child has good in him, has potentialities that can be realized, and is worth the thought and the effort involved in helping him. Someone must feel that a child is worth the bother he causes before he can ever really believe in himself.[9]

An illuminating incident regarding this type of action was reported by a principal:

> Early in spring I received notice that a noted troublemaker from another school in our district was being transferred to our school. He was a seventh-grade boy, very mature, and big for his age. I called Bill into my office the first day and told him I was very happy to see him

at our school. I told him we could use a boy like him for our patrol and also that he would be a definite asset to our softball team. I knew ahead of time that he was a good athlete and liked baseball. I also talked a little baseball with him, and I could see he was happy with our little conversation.

Bill was placed on the patrol and has done an excellent job. He has been guilty of a few minor rule infractions but has done nothing seriously wrong. He is very well liked by his classmates, and he has become a leader with his peer group.

I have become quite fond of Bill and consider him one of the nicest boys attending the school. His mother recently came to school and told me how happy she was about the way Bill has been behaving himself and how much he likes to come to school.

Here we see a principal taking positive action. He does not make assumptions regarding the boy's past reputation but picks out his assets and focuses on them. He shows his belief that Bill has something good in him and acts as if he really expects a good relationship.

The results reported in both behavior and attitude change illustrate well the efficacy of this approach to a child who was considered difficult.

Showing Faith in the Child

In another incident we see a teacher who seizes the opportunity to transmit her belief in an individual.

The children were sitting on the floor of the library at school listening to the librarian tell about the Caldecott and Newberry awards. The librarian was explaining that the Caldecott was awarded for the best illustrated children's book of the year. Mrs. Smith, the teacher, said, "Some of you children may grow up to be fine book illustrators and perhaps achieve this award some day." Tim spoke up and said that he had just written a story and he bet he could draw a picture for every page, and win an award too, right now. Instead of doing what some might consider the obvious and pointing out that he was too young, that he would have to grow up and work hard at his art before this could happen, Mrs. Smith agreed with him, saying that he was a fine artist and that his work was very good.

Another teacher might have preached about the virtues of hard work, sacrifice, and school. She would have detailed the long path toward adulthood and maturity. Instead, Mrs. Smith took the opportunity to recognize what Tim does well. He is capable in art, and she used his proficiency to encourage. She recognized his present achievement, showed her satisfaction with it, and led him to believe in his capacities.

Creating Self-Confidence Through Faith in the Child

One needs not only to show faith, but to be convincing enough to develop faith in the child. The teacher must solidly communicate the "I know you can do it" attitude.

> The first grade was presenting a program for the other grades. The program was a play which involved some reading. The best readers were chosen for the leading roles. The day before the program many of the children were not in school because of illness. The teacher had to find replacements. Danny was a boy who never read in class. He did not like to read and never read well. The teacher took this opportunity to stimulate him. She said, "Danny, would you like to take the reading part? We need someone who can do a good job, and I am sure you can."
>
> Danny was reluctant. Tryouts were scheduled for lunch hour. At lunch time Danny was there. He was not the best reader, but the teacher told him he read well. The teacher helped Danny after school, and Danny took the play home to practice. The next day on the program Danny was an effective reader replacement. He had an opportunity to attain real social status, to belong. He felt successful when the play was a success. From that day on Danny loved to read and volunteered frequently in the classroom.

Recognizing a Job Well Done and Giving Recognition for Effort

Children sometimes persuade teachers that they cannot function. The teachers are surprised to learn the real capabilities of the child once proper recognition is given.

> Tommy had been a problem all year in many ways. Because he failed to turn in arithmetic assignments, he had been held back from going on to multiplication with the rest of the group. He appeared to accept this calmly and continued to function in the same manner, until one day I gave a test including addition, subtraction, and multiplication. He was instructed to do only the first two parts. Much to my amazement he did part three and did it exceptionally well! I praised him highly in front of all, and soon the children too were encouraging him. Tommy functioned effectively in arithmetic from that point on.

Here we are exposed to the importance of recognition. The teacher wisely chose to believe in Tommy. She acted prudently and gave full recognition to his effort. Children can be influenced positively when teachers react at the "teachable moment."

Utilizing the Group

We assume that all behavior has social meaning and that one of the child's prime purposes is to belong. Awareness of this goal suggests that the teacher use the group for the optimal development of the individual. In the ensuing incident the teacher used the seating arrangement of the classroom.

> I rearranged the seating in the classroom early in April. One of the changes was placing Ruth and John next to each other.
>
> Ruth is a somewhat withdrawn child who does above average in her school work. She is an avid reader and has an extensive personal library which includes a variety of science and history books for young children. Many of these books are kept in school either in Ruth's desk or in her locker. All of her spare time is spent reading books. Her social contacts are almost nonexistent.
>
> John is an active, outgoing boy, somewhat of a discipline problem. He is slightly below average in achievement. The apparent cause of poor achievement is his inattentiveness combined with a desire to finish, regardless of quality, all he is assigned.
>
> Within a few days after the change in seating, I noticed that John asked Ruth about a book she was reading. She passed it to him, and John started to look through it, making a comment now and then and calling her attention to a picture. I walked past their desks and saw that it was a book about the planets. Soon Ruth was letting John borrow her books. He has been spending a lot of time reading both in school and at home. Recently, I saw Ruth and John talking outside after school. The children tell me they walk home together almost every day.

Here we note the teacher used two personalities to supplement each other's development. This judicious use of seating arrangements, which showed an awareness of the importance of sociometrics, could benefit many children.

Integrating the Group

Teachers need an awareness of individual differences. Variances in rate of development interest, and capacity need to be accounted for in planning and carrying out instructions. However, attention must be given to the group. The teacher must frequently direct herself to the task of dealing with the group. The following is a story about a small group working at a special problem.

I have nine boys and one girl from grades 6, 7, and 8 working alone in an extra room from 2:00 to 2:45 p.m. daily. All but one have serious reading handicaps. One asked to join the class for self-improvement. I gave them a talk describing the self-study and test program. They believe in the program implicitly. One eighth-grade boy, who does not cry readily, burst into tears when they returned to their home room. The eighth-grade teacher asked what happened. "I got six wrong," said Bill.

I do not ask their scores, as this is a private project. Next day I had two minutes alone with Bill. "Why don't you ask me for help if you don't know how to answer a question?" I asked.

"In front of those sixth-grade kids?" answered Bill.

"They are doing easier cards than you are, but I'll step into the hall with you if you'd rather. What gave you trouble?" I asked.

"Those long and short marks; I can't tell the difference," replied Bill.

"Well, thank you for telling me. Maybe there are a lot of others in your room who can't. I'll have Mrs. James explain it for all the grade in English class tomorrow," I promised.

Here the teacher took the children to a place where they could work at their own level. She showed faith in them by leaving them alone. Responsibility was shared, and learning proceeded.

Assist in the Development of Skills Sequentially and Psychologically Paced to Permit Success

Part of teaching consists of being alert to what the child is currently able to achieve.

Millie is a slow learner. She is a fifth-grade girl who was a member of a club for girls which I helped to direct. A part of the club work is memorizing. The girls have booklets with sections on which they are tested and for which they receive awards similar to the scouting program. In most cases the girls learned the verses at home and just recited them to the leaders at the club meeting. Millie was having trouble. She couldn't seem to pass any of the work. I realized she needed encouragement.

I went over with Millie the particular section she had to do and said to her, "Now you study just this much, and then say it to me."

When she had learned one small part, we went on to the next little bit. After she had learned each assigned portion to the end of the section, I had her look over the whole section again. She was then able to recite the whole section. Millie was a very happy girl when I was able to sign the section indicating that she had passed it. After that meeting, Millie did not sit with a baffled look on her face. It had seemed like an insurmountable task to her. Now she knew that she

could do it. Millie gained courage through pacing. This technique can
be applied to groups also.

I have found that the best form of encouragement is never to let
a child fail in his efforts. I have physical education classes and use this
method all the time. Some children are better than others in certain
activities; some cannot perform at all. In my instruction I keep up a
constant line of sincere praise. I tell each child how well he did; when
someone is so wrong that the whole class knows it, I always find a part
to praise. If the child receives such praise he does not tense up, and
even though he is not good, he will return for more instruction and
will soon do the job well enough. It frequently happens that the
other children also take pride in this child's progress.

Here the teacher's philosophy is geared to sincere praise. The
children function more effectively when they are paced sequentially
and when the correct part is recognized.

Recognizing and Focusing
on Strengths and Assets

Teachers are inclined to feel it is their duty to point out mistakes. They frequently consider diagnosing errors as the major concern. If the relationship with a child is primarily one of pointing
out mistakes, the relationship will obviously not be a pleasant one.
Adequate learning requires concentration on what is correct along
with awareness of errors. It is suggested that much can be gained
from consciously seeking each individual's assets. It would be worth
while for each teacher at the start of each year to determine each
child's greatest asset. When we know the child's major asset, our
relationship can be improved.

George did not do any class assignments. He had an average I.Q.
After about three weeks of school had passed, I discovered that he
could read very well. I brought this ability to the front and allowed
George to experience success in this area, and it wasn't long before he
started trying in the other subjects. His status in the group ascended
rapidly.

This teacher found the boy's strength and through concentration on it helped his general adjustment and achievement.

Footnotes

[1] Dreikurs, *Psychology,* p. 23.

[2] Daniel A. Prescott, *The Child in the Educative Process* (New York: McGraw-Hill Book Company, Inc., 1957), p. 153.

[3] Chester Harris, ed., *Encyclopedia of Educational Research,* 3rd ed. (New York: The Macmillan Company, 1960), p. 898.

[4] Edith G. Neisser, *How to Live with Children* (Chicago: Science Research Association, 1950).

[5] Mabel Morphett and Carleton Washburne, *Postponing Formal Instruction: A Seven-Year Case Study, in the Effect of Administrative Practices on the Character of the Education Program-Symposium* (Washington, D.C.: American Educational Research Association, 1940).

[6] Rudolf Dreikurs, "Emotional Predispositions to Reading Difficulties," *Archives of Pediatrics,* Vol. 71, 339-353, November 1954.

[7] H. Bakwin and R. Bakwin, *Clinical Management of Behavior Disorders in Children,* 2nd ed. (Philadelphia: W. B. Saunders, 1960).

[8] Rudolf Dreikurs, Raymond Corsini, Raymond Lowe, and Manford Sonstegard. *Adlerian Family Counseling* (Eugene, Oregon: University of Oregon Press, 1959), p. 23.

[9] Prescott, *Child,* p. 73.

five | *Encouragement in Specific Fields*

Up to now we have discussed encouragement as a philosophy and as a general technique and have given examples of the use of encouragement in a variety of situations.

The teacher who adopts this approach needs to understand the general philosophy underlying encouragement. Valuing, showing faith, stimulating belief in self, giving recognition for effort, utilizing the group to enhance development, pacing, and a recognition of and focus on strengths, assets, and interests are all basic principles. Positive methods will dominate the teacher's relationship with children in an atmosphere that is encouraging and stimulating. Children will function more effectively because they will regularly be presented with appropriate tasks. They will be accepted for what they accomplish, regardless of its extent, and will not be judged punitively. In this environment nurture will occur with relative freedom from deprivation. The mistake-centered classroom will be eliminated as the teacher sees the result of the new relationship.

However, specific techniques are needed to handle the various situations that arise. In this section we shall develop and illustrate some specific situations involving encouragement.

57

Developing Skills

Our concern with developing skills requires the development of processes which will lead to easy and efficient performances. This involves more than merely the motor behavior; it includes a variety of skills like athletic ability, playing an instrument, typing, English usage, and games. Essentially, it involves a complex integration of processes resulting in manipulative ability.

Encouragement is necessary for the child's development. He becomes what he is encouraged to become. Teachers must be made aware of the importance of assisting the child to his optimal development within his social setting.

Encouragement stimulates the child to do his best and enables him to recognize his abilities. The process of encouragement then extends beyond mere faith and belief in the individual to include the capacity for translating this faith and belief to the child. The child may not be perfect in his performance, but commending him on his effort enables him to grow through belief in himself and his abilities.

Encouragement in skills can occur in a variety of areas. The following examples enable us to see simple ways of developing skills through encouragement.

A physical-education class at the third-grade level. The children are selecting four team captains. The first three were selected quickly. Then, after a pause, Nancy was nominated. Nancy was of adequate physique but was recognized as shy and sensitive. The nomination had really been made to put Nancy in an uncomfortable position.

Nancy's immediate response was delight at what she misinterpreted as friendliness. However, her extreme shyness and her recognition of the lack of good motor skills quickly made her hesitant. She said, "Oh no, not me. I'm not good enough."

The teacher recognized the situation and moved in by saying, "Yes, Nancy, I think you would be a good captain." The election was soon over. The teacher quickly gave Nancy some additional coaching. Nancy came to believe in her skills, and the team performed well. The other girls almost seemed to sense that they should make up for what had originally been a rather cruel act.

Comment: Here the teacher took command of a situation which could have been harmful for Nancy's development, in that it could have reinforced her feelings of incompetence, and used it to her advantage. His attention and belief in Nancy permitted the other children to see her in a new light.

> Billy, age nine, was new in the neighborhood. He soon had an opportunity to enter a neighborhood ball game. His lack of skill and experience was soon evident, and many quarrels took place about why Billy should not be on one team or the other. This only focused on Billy's inadequate skills. He soon withdrew from such activity and would find excuses not to go out when baseball was being played.
>
> Billy's father recognized the lack of skill and found time to play with Billy in the yard. However, more frequently than not Billy dropped the ball or missed it when batting. He would suggest, "Let's do something else."
>
> Father believed Billy could learn, and he purchased a ball large enough and soft enough for Billy to succeed. He himself threw and pitched the ball very carefully so that some success was highly probable. He always commended successful efforts and noted the good parts of tries that did not end in success. Billy's faith in himself was slowly restored. Shortly, the father did not need to try so hard to insure success. It was not too long before the skills were being used in neighborhood games.

Comment: Proper diagnosis permitted the father to see the discouragement in Billy. Patience permitted him to start where Billy could succeed. Recognition enabled the boy to believe in himself.

Young children are particularly amenable to improvement through encouragement. Frequently their lack of skill may be related to fears and discouragement.

This report deals with overcoming a child's fear, in this case the fear of water.

> Virginia, age 26 months, had become afraid of water as a result of rough play and splashing by older children, mainly around a neighbor's pool. Virginia was affected to such an extent that she cried even when confronted with sticking her toes in the water.
>
> I took it upon myself to help this child forget her fear of water so that she could enjoy herself in a pool or lake. The first thing that I did was to take Virginia to the pool in the absence of other children. While I went for a swim, Virginia began running from side to side. I could see that she was interested in getting wet and playing. Through a series of steps paced to her readiness, I let her dangle her fingers in the water and then her feet; finally I let her climb down and sit on the ladder with her feet in the water. I realized that patience would be a big factor in stimulating this child to lose fear. When she re-

sisted I abandoned the process for a short time and never teased the
child into the water.

Through this gradual process I saw Virginia come to the point
where now she will put on a float and will really enjoy herself in the
shallow end of the pool. Her fear has been overcome through encouragement, and I feel a sense of satisfaction in knowing that I may
have been of some help to this child.

Comment: Virginia had come to interpret the water as a source of
few satisfactions. Through the patience and understanding of the
adult she came to see that she could succeed. One needs to allow
the child to experience success in order to overcome fear.

A number of the skills more closely related to success in school
need to be viewed in a new manner for the child to function effectively. Pointing out errors and mistakes is not as helpful as striking
upon the facet of the skill that the child can perform.

> Sally is a sixth grader who comes to my class for reading, lan-
> guage arts, and arithmetic. She has been quite resistant to the exactness
> required by spelling and arithmetic. Not only did she do poorly, but
> frequently no work was completed to permit evaluation. During the
> study period I have had her assist me in correcting spelling and arith-
> metic papers. I give her a sample which she compares with the other
> papers. She appears to enjoy this and now also shows more interest
> and does her work completely.

Comment: The teacher did something simple but most effective
here. Traditionally she might have assumed that since Sally could
not complete her work she could not do anything else less difficult.
However, no fuss was made over Sally's inadequacies; instead, the
teacher enlisted her assistance. The child was impressed with the
responsibility placed upon her in this situation. The teacher's faith
enabled Sally to believe in her own capacities.

> Tim, age eleven, had considerable difficulty in arithmetic because
> he was weak in fundamentals, particularly in multiplication tables.
> I involved Tim in making a chart that quickly revealed the tables and
> answers. Later he brought it to my desk. I commented, "My, this is a
> good job, and I know several children that need one. Could you help
> me and make some for them?" The next day Tim arrived in class with
> four additional charts. I thanked him and used the charts appropri-
> ately. Tim's difficulty with this phase of arithmetic fundamentals dis-
> appeared as a result of the practice he had while constructing the
> charts.

Comment: Effective teaching requires the ability to take advantage of incidents that are timely. The teacher saw an opportunity for Tim to be useful and to be helped at the same time. Assigned as drill work, the task would have been completed grudgingly and with little lasting benefit. Doing a job that benefited others and permitted Tim to be useful gave him a sense of belonging and contributing. A situation that permitted Tim to function with respect brought mastery of the skill.

IMPROVING LEARNING

Reading

Reading is basic to most academic tasks. The application of sound principles of encouragement is particularly needed here to assist the discouraged child.

> Billy, age eleven, has an I.Q. well above average but is retarded several years in reading. In tutoring I began with material appropriate to the level of his present achievement. We also printed up stories that he made up, and he learned to read them. Simple games involving reading were played. Billy began to experience success in various activities. His attitude became one of confidence as he attacked the advancing levels of comprehension. I spent little time detailing errors and at each step was careful to commend progress and in general support his efforts.

Comment: The tutor began with materials at the appropriate level. She focused on Billy's strengths. By her belief that he was doing his best Billy found courage to take the varied developmental steps.

> Danny, grade 5, started having difficulty in reading after having done satisfactory work in the earlier grades. The teacher indicated, a few weeks after school started, that Danny would not pass. He reacted by becoming anxious and developing into a behavior problem. The teacher in turn reacted to this by keeping him in his seat writing various statements one hundred times. His achievement test score sank to the second-grade level. Danny was failed and retained at the close of the school year. A former teacher was asked to tutor Danny during the summer. She started by finding the boy's current level of achievement. Then she found some stories in areas where he had expressed an interest. Danny was interested in learning what happened in each story; in the process basic skills were developed. At the end of the summer tutoring session another achievement test was given and

Danny scored at the sixth-grade level. The principal, after an examination of the evidence and upon the tutor's recommendation, ad-
vanced Danny to sixth grade. Danny was most pleased, and reacted
with both good achievement and constructive behavior.

Comment: The first teacher showed openly her lack of faith in
Danny's ability. She adopted a punitive approach for getting him
back into line. This resulted in more misbehavior and lowered
achievement. The tutor found the key through interest and work
at which Danny could succeed. Recognition was given for effort.
Skills were absorbed but in the child's mind were secondary to the
fun of knowing what happened in the story. In her approach to the
problem and in the special effort she made to see the principal
about Danny's status, the tutor showed that she valued the child.
The principal showed his faith in the boy by promoting him into
the proper grade. This belief in Danny facilitated the boy's capacity
to believe in his own functioning.

Gerry, now in the eighth grade, had always been one of the youngest in his class. His immaturity and lack of confidence early caused
teachers to be concerned about promotion and retention. The parents
felt strongly that Gerry should not be kept back. Parents and relatives
always compared Gerry with a more successful cousin, supposedly as a
stimulant. It only brought about a greater lack of confidence, stutter-
ing, and withdrawal from the reading task. Gerry early in his academic
life became discouraged about the possibility of his achieving success
in reading. He felt unsuccessful and whatever attention he received
focused on his inadequacies. Even yearly summer-school attendance
was interpreted by Gerry as an annual affirmation of his inabilities.

A diagnostic appraisal by the psychologist showed Gerry to be
average in intelligence and achieving at around the third-grade level
in reading. Personality testing revealed a number of feelings of inadequacy. Among other things, a successful younger sister was a problem that hindered Gerry. The better she was, the less able he was to
compete with her academically. His place in life came from trying to
please and by displaying inadequacy. He saw himself as living with
problems bigger than he was able to solve. Dependency on mother
was great.

Gerry began educational therapy in a setting that attended to the
total difficulty. Materials with a teen-age interest level but a grade
level below his competence, were assigned. He began with little faith
in his capacities. It was pointed out to Gerry that the therapist felt
he could do the job and that he needed to decide for himself if it was
worth the effort. Gerry took some self-testing material home and soon

came to feel that he could help himself. At the next meeting he was quite pleased and encouraged by his success. He asked for more homework than the first time. Over a period of several months steady effort by Gerry and its recognition by the therapist brought slow but sure success. Soon he could read and participate more adequately in some of the regular classroom work. New recognition from his group enhanced the development of his reading ability.

Comment: Gerry's teachers probably were alerted early to some of the developmental problems. The parents caused the boy to be placed where opportunity for success was quite restricted. Comparisons with the cousin lessened self-esteem and faith in himself. Winning attention for not succeeding soon became just as rewarding as continuing the struggle.

Adequate diagnosis helped determine the child's potential and his present achievement. The therapist's faith enabled Gerry to make the attempt. His experience with the material made him believe he could succeed. The new-found status in the group satisfied his basic need to belong. Focus was placed on what Gerry could do, and he became aware of certain assets.

Darrell, age twelve, retained in school several times, now in grade four. His approach to school work was to do as little as possible. The home situation was confusing and discipline inconsistent. Teacher control of Darrell came through making him write statements several hundred times and keeping him in at recess.

Diagnostic testing placed Darrell's I.Q. in the normal range. Achievement tests found Darrell achieving at about the third-grade level. Personality testing showed Darrell to be discouraged and pessimistic with little sense of personal worth. Feelings of inadequacy and of the futility of striving were present.

In educational therapy Darrell again showed resistance to finishing materials. Baby talk and mumbling were mechanisms used to avoid work and problems. His characteristic approach to homework was to accept as little as possible and to forget to do it or to bring it to the therapist.

Some interpretation of his purposes was made to Darrell. He was given work at his level of achievement. Darrell began to do some work and was commended for all constructive efforts. Stress was placed on forming a good relationship with the therapist. Through a period of several months progress and regression occurred as Darrell continued to have problems with the punitive approach in school and with the lack of consistency and warm relationships at home. Retesting eventually showed Darrell achieving at fifth-grade level.

Comment: This indicates well why a total approach must be adopted toward problems of the individual. Factors in the school and home prevented Darrell from making big strides. What helped Darrell make the progress he did? First, he was sincerely and consistently valued by the therapist. Punitive methods were avoided. Material at the proper level was presented. Faith in Darrell's ability was always shown.

Spelling

This subject provides an opportunity to observe children who resist order and their characteristic pattern in dealing with order. Spelling demands accuracy and precision. If one does not want to cooperate with the required order, spelling provides an area of resistance.

> Martin had not learned any of his spelling words during the first two months of the semester. One day when he could not respond, I told him that he should listen to the next child and that I would come back to him. On the third try he made it. "That's fine, Martin, come to the blackboard," I said. When I asked him to write the word, he said he could not. Again a child spelled the word, and Martin repeated it; each time he made a mistake the class responded for him. At last I asked him to write the word, and he did. After many repetitions he wrote four words. Each time he got a word correct, I praised him. The class started out laughing at him but ended up supporting him. The next step I used was to erase, one at a time, his written words, asking him to repeat them. As he got the first word right we went on to the second. At the second word I went back to the first word. At the third word we repeated the other two words several times. By the fourth word I switched all four words around. I then sent him to his seat and had the whole class write the four words and the previous day's words. When Martin said he could not do those, I told him I expected him to write only the four words we had worked on. As we were getting ready to go home, he came up to me and presented me with one of his animal erasers. "Here, I want you to have this."

Comment: The teacher recognized that Martin lacked courage and belief in his capacities. She began with a situation in which the possibilities of success were extremely high. She quickly enlisted the support of the class to enhance Martin's development. By expecting of Martin only what she knew he was capable of accomplishing, she did not permit failure to occur, even after the experience was completed. Any opportunity to display inadequacy was removed.

Dan, aged nine, enjoyed most of his school work but functioned ineffectively in spelling. His approach was one of, "I just can't get that stuff." Various solutions were tried until mother got the idea of a family paper. Dan liked to read and to tell about his experiences. Writing was one of his favorite activities. A staff for the home paper was formed. Dan was appointed editor, and soon articles were being submitted. He was to correct and approve all copy. Pride in his responsibilities caused him to look at all copy carefully and make corrections. Soon the problem of spelling accuracy disappeared.

Comment: An opportunity to use the skill in an endeavor Dan could really become involved in was presented. The family's faith in Dan was illustrated by his selection as editor and chief copy reader. This faith enabled him to believe he could develop the skill. His place in the group was strengthened through the important function he performed.

Penmanship

Tim does well in creative work but is apt to be in such a hurry that his writing is messy. For an American history assignment, he wrote a poem about Captain John Smith which was so good that each of the other fifth-grade classes wanted a copy. Thrilled by this recognition, Tim made three very neat copies for them.

Comment: The work took on a new significance in that there was a real purpose for its being readable. His significance in the group was used to lead him to value penmanship. The teacher focused on his asset, the creative work, and seized the opportunity to let him recognize for himself the value of neat work.

I had a left-handed girl in my room who was very self-conscious and discouraged about her penmanship. Mary held her paper and arm in a very peculiar position, and this induced poor writing habits and letter formation. Being left-handed, I understood her problem although I never had experienced a "twisted" arm or poor writing. I helped her on the blackboard before school started and also showed her how to use and hold her pencil correctly. Her penmanship improved, and I sought opportunities for her to use this skill in helping me put materials on the board. She soon gained self-confidence about her penmanship.

Comment: The teacher valued Mary and gave her additional time. She showed her faith in Mary, as skill progressed, by letting her assist at the board. This also allowed the group to help Mary by recognizing her work.

Mathematics

I had Sam in seventh grade. He had a low I.Q., was overage and very large, and read on a fourth-grade level. He felt inferior to the group. I worked with Sam by giving him very simple tasks, and he was successful to the extent that he began to feel some measure of acceptance. One could see that he felt more at ease in the group. Sam worked in his uncle's grocery store after school. I used him in arithmetic class as a source of reference for the prices of food, etc. He felt very assured because he knew something the rest of us did not know as well.

Comment: This teacher, though confronted with a variety of handicaps to the learning task, started at the level where she felt Sam could succeed. This permitted group acceptance to take place. She focused on his one asset in mathematics. The knowledge of grocery prices gave him a real place of significance.

Ronald had great difficulty in learning his arithmetic families. Finally he almost mastered how they worked. Salvador entered our class and did not understand the arithmetic families at all. Ronald was asked to help Salvador. When Salvador started to understand the arithmetic families, Ronald was so encouraged by Salvador's improvement that he developed renewed interest himself.

Comment: The opportunity to work with another child and see him develop built up Ronald's confidence in his own capacities. It also gave him a chance to function in a constructive manner.

Science

George did poor work in science class. Observation revealed that he worked very capably with his hands. George was made project chairman for our class, which put him in charge of planning and construction for all our science projects. Among his achievements was a papier-mâché volcano, elaborately painted and showing inside layers. George's grades showed improvement through his newly found position.

Comment: This teacher was not limited by the academic field in searching for ways to value George and enhance his status in the group. The opportunity to use a strength enabled him to function in a number of areas.

> Bill, seventh grade, did poorly in our science class. One day I discovered that he made frequent trips with his uncle on a large diesel truck. I asked Bill if he could explain the principle of this operation to our class. He was sure he could. Soon we had a most interesting discussion which culminated in the uncle's coming to the school grounds to demonstrate the operation of the truck. Bill had a new place in our group, and this stimulated him to work more studiously on the other parts of the science course.

Comment: The teacher saw that Bill's experience outside of school was a real asset. She maximized this advantage by giving him a chance to find increased status. When we work from the asset first, instead of focusing and drilling on the weakness, we permit our faith and confidence to strengthen the child's convictions about his capacities and to alter his mistaken assumptions about his limitations.

SOCIAL SCIENCE

> David used the social-science period to distract the other children and annoy the teacher. He said, "There is no use in learning all that old stuff about what used to happen." The children were studying the formation of the Constitution and decided they would like to make a constitution. David said his father knew all about how you make rules since he worked at the court. The father had specialized in the study of constitutions as part of his work. David had the opportunity to bring examples of various constitutions and contribute materials of significance to the project.

Comment: David's original participation was just in the area where he was knowledgeable. The improvement in his status should lead him to expand in other directions.

> Sarah had little interest in the history course. It did not seem to solve any problem she was interested in. One day the teacher mentioned the great variety of clothing fads through the years. Sarah was attracted to the idea and later asked if she might do a project on this topic. At first the teacher questioned the value of this study in relation to the broad field being studied, but granted permission. Sarah soon collected information about clothing from many periods of history. In the course of her study she encountered many facts about

the customs of people and nations and learned much about the various historical periods.

Comment: Begin with the child's interest, even though at the time it may not appear directly related to your goal. Show the child that you feel his project has importance. Integration of her project with class goals will occur as relationships develop.

> Geography class held little excitement for Eddie. His thoughts were directed toward ball playing and other out-of-class interests. He became very difficult to manage in class and was particularly obnoxious about correcting the teacher on certain facts regarding the western states. The surety with which he stated his case led the teacher to suspect that he had some special knowledge of the area. A check of her facts found Eddie correct in each instance. Further investigation produced the information that Eddie had traveled extensively in the west during summer vacations and that the family had a large collection of pictures and souvenirs. He was invited to bring materials to class. The pictures brought new insight into the geographical study. Eddie's value to the class was obvious. The teacher gave adequate recognition, and Eddie decided to investigate other areas of geography just as thoroughly as he had the west.

Comment: The teacher did not allow her relationship to the pupil to be affected by the fact that she had been incorrect about some of the class material. She investigated and learned how Eddie could be an asset to her course. By permitting Eddie to succeed he was able to improve his relationship to the course and the teacher as well.

Art

> Eight-year-old Johnny approached the teacher's desk with a drawing marked "fair" clutched in his hand. The teacher knew that Johnny had expended a great deal of effort, interest, and imagination on this particular drawing; in other words, he had done his best. His best evidently had not been good enough as far as the art teacher was concerned. Johnny was disappointed, discouraged, and close to tears. The teacher pointed out the better parts of the drawing. Then she suggested how it might be improved with heavier strokes here, an addition of colors there, and a bit more detail as far as the figures were concerned. She said she felt it was the best picture he had ever done. In his free time Johnny followed her suggestions and handed in the improved drawing to the art teacher. It was returned marked "excellent," and Johnny beamed with pride.

Comment: The good parts of the picture were mentioned first. Johnny's efforts were recognized, and he could reapproach the task confident that there was value in his work.

After examining several of Janet's attempts at drawing, I found I needed to praise and encourage her sincerely so that she would not lose interest. She was thus inspired to do several little art projects and began sincerely to enjoy art. Because I first commended her she gained confidence and was enabled to examine her own art work critically, which helped her to improve. The child now accepts not only praise but also constructive criticism without any feelings of inferiority about her art skills.

Comment: Begin where the child is and value that project. Give him strength so that he can eventually be critical of his own materials.

Speech

Ann was five and a half when she entered kindergarten. Her speech pattern was so poor that any word using s, th, sh, l, d, r, w, v, and f was so mispronounced that it was unintelligible. She walked with her head down, seldom spoke to anyone, pretended not to hear, and was most antisocial. Her ability to follow directions was excellent.

As the children were leaving for home one day, several hangers left on the floor gave me an opening to ask her help. We came to know each other well. I began speech assistance with the aid of a mirror. I showed her where to place the tongue. Folding the tongue in half she would work on like, love, let, etc. I never nagged, just persisted. Once a month we used the tape recorder. Each tape was kept. I used vanity, too; she had lovely blue eyes, and I asked her why she didn't let her friends see how beautiful they were. I explained that if she didn't want to talk, she could smile with her eyes.

When I was sure she knew the answer to a question I asked, I called on her. By Christmas she was giving small responses. She gave a short piece with another child at the close of the school year. She continued with a speech lesson once a week for another year. Ann is now in fourth grade, a delightful little chatterbox. The tape recordings are the only evidence of speech difficulty.

Comment: Several encouragement techniques were employed. Ann was made a useful member of the group. An asset, her appearance, was commended. She was called on in situations where success was quite certain.

DEVELOPING ATTITUDINAL PROCESSES

The school must take responsibility for more than the purely academic. It is responsible for helping to influence the way children feel about a variety of topics and problems. The child's attitude predisposes him to act in a certain manner. Any influence on attitudes is crucial because it so closely relates to the motivational set of the individual.

The emotional climate of the room and the interaction between teacher and pupil are important areas to be considered.

> One year a boy with a reputation of being very difficult to handle was assigned to my room. He had spent the last year in the principal's office, half of the time in the hall. His record indicated about thirty tardy marks.
>
> On the day the report cards were distributed showing room assignments, David came charging into my room and, with a "Boy, you're sure stuck with me attitude" shouted, "Mrs. Miller, I'm going to be in your room. Now, what do you think of that?" I looked at the boy and quietly said, "I know, David. I asked for you." His face lighted up from ear to ear, and I know he was completely shocked. It was safe to assume he had never been "asked for" before, because his name meant trouble as did the name of his family. My reply was totally unexpected, and I am sure it encouraged David to know he was wanted. As he bolted out of the room, he shouted, "See you next year."

Comment: The teacher in a simple act changed the entire atmosphere. She threw David off balance at first because she did the unexpected; then her complete acceptance caused him to feel he could get along with this teacher. Not much time was involved, but the relationship was clearly established.

> Diane, a seven-year-old second grader had been a problem since she entered school. She hit children, threw all available objects, screamed, and ran around the classroom. She usually refused to enter into activities—individual or group, academic or recreational. While reading poetry to the class, I noticed an enraptured look on her face. I asked her if she wanted to read some poetry. She read for me and for each class. The children praised her and asked her to enter their activities. This helped her confidence and her reading.

Comment: The teacher looked closely to find, even in a passive moment, some opportunity to assist Diane. She took advantage of the interest to absorb the child into the group and to cause her to focus on constructive activity.

Jackie, in second grade, had a "growing up" problem. He misbehaved everywhere and then went home to his mother for sympathy. However, she was not free of his bad behavior. He disturbed her continuously. He had made his first-grade teacher miserable for the entire year. I had had Jackie in kindergarten. He had kept things in turmoil there as much as he could. However, he knew and remembered that I liked a quiet, peaceful room. With this in the back of his mind, he had grown up enough to believe he could make me conform to his way of thinking and let him do as he pleased in order to have peace.

For several days he won. His special teachers didn't know what to do with him. The principal couldn't reach him. He insisted on going where he pleased. If I asked him to behave he screamed and cried and said he hated me. I showed no reaction to his tantrums but always made him a leader or let him paint or made him a helper for a slower child, whenever he was cooperative.

The children in the room were very cooperative. He developed very rapidly and learned to enjoy all of us. Now, even after two years, his mother thanks me over and over for my patience with Jackie.

Comment: This teacher will not be intimidated into a power contest or struggle for control. She rewards appropriate behavior and refuses to become annoyed with disturbances. The child comes up against someone who is his match. At each stage where he functions effectively encouragement is applied.

Bobby, age five, was continually involved in fights during playtime in the kindergarten. In each situation he strove to obtain the teacher's assistance by complaining about the other children and their treatment of him. I told him the fights were his problem and refused to become involved as an arbitrator. One day he brought some toys the other children wanted to play with. I stepped in to show them how all could share. Bobby was impressed with his new-found esteem and soon found greater rewards in this behavior than in his former attitude.

Comment: The teacher took the moment that provided the greatest opportunity for Bobby to develop sound social attitudes and turned it into a triumph. Good teaching looks for important moments that need the reinforcement of the teacher's approval. Certainly Bobby's integration into the group and belonging aided his development materially.

Facilitating Social Adjustment

The social functioning of the child is also the concern of the school. There is a basic need to belong. The teacher's awareness of this primary need should assist in explaining some classroom behavior. We have long insisted that teachers recognize individual differences and deal with the problems of the individual. Now there must be renewed recognition of the importance of training the teacher to deal with the group. The group has a vital relationship to the functioning of the individual. Status in the group and the forming of wholesome relationships concern the child. Overt lack of concern may only serve as a symptom of mental-health difficulties.

The child should be in the process of moving from dependence to independence. This implies fewer demands on the parental figures. At the same time the teacher needs to lead the child to recognize the importance of interaction and interdependence. The classroom provides many opportunities to focus on the advantages of working together. Cooperation and social interest are fundamental to developing the proper group spirit and group atmosphere.

The child's concerns in social-emotional areas may influence his effectiveness with subject matter as well as with people.

The atmosphere of the group has been proved to have a definite effect on the kinds of behavior children produce. Lewin, Lippitt, and White are responsible for basic studies related to understanding social climates or group atmospheres.[1] Using three types of control characterized as authoritarian, democratic, and laissez-faire, they found that more friendly remarks and fewer expressions of discontent occurred in the democratic group.

The atmosphere and general management of the classroom situation can serve not only to promote more productive work but also to enhance and facilitate social adjustment.

One of the points at which the teacher can begin is in her general organization of the group. Here a teacher describes a system of room organization that proved effective for her.

> An extremely effective method of giving children status in the classroom and among other children in the school and at home is through the organizational setup of a class club.
> We elect four officers, president, vice president, secretary, and treasurer. The duties of the president are to conduct class for fifteen minutes each morning except Fridays when the vice president takes

over. The vice president also conducts class when the president is absent. The secretary writes class thank-you notes, invitations, etc. The treasurer collects money for drives, etc. No child may hold one of these major offices twice until each child in the room has had a turn. After seven months of school, if there are twenty-eight children in a room and elections are held once a month, the elections are thrown open to all the children for a second round.

Comment: This is a simple but direct way of developing cooperation and participation while providing status for the children in a variety of situations. The organization provides for more harmonious group living and at the same time attends to the individual's need to belong.

Lowell, a very bright (I.Q. 141) but very aggressive boy in the classroom and on the playground (always in a fight), had been placed in my room because he was unable to adjust to the other sixth-grade teacher. Lowell had two brothers, one nine years older and one thirteen years older with whom he shared a room but who constantly pushed him around mentally and physically. Lowell was asked to help three boys in the room with their school work. This gave him a feeling of doing something worth while instead of just being the youngest and most ineffective as he was at home. Lowell was able to have fewer flare-ups in the room, nor did he seem to have the need to explode as much on the playground.

Comment: The teacher used her knowledge of the family constellation to make her aware of possible explanations of the boy's behavior. Then she did not talk about what to do but took action. The faith she revealed and the responsibility Lowell accepted placed him in a new relationship to his classmates.

Footnotes

[1] Kurt Lewin, Ronald Lippitt, and R. K. White, "Patterns of Aggressive Behavior in Experimentally Created 'Social Climates,'" *Journal of Social Psychology* 10 (1939), 271-299, and Ronald Lippitt, "Studies in Topological and Vector Psychology in an Experimental Study of Effects of Democratic and Authoritarian Group Atmospheres," *University of Iowa Studies in Child Welfare*, Vol. 16, No. 3, 1940.

six | # *Personal and Social Adjustment Through Encouragement*

We have discussed the use of encouragement to facilitate development in a variety of academic areas. However, encouragement can also assist development in the personal-social areas.

Development of the Self-Concept

The self-concept here will refer to the individual's personal perceptions, his view of life and of himself. These are the convictions he holds about self. While others may consider these convictions to be fallacious, they make sense to him at this time and underlie his actions.

Our responses are influenced by our experiences in the past and by our anticipation of the future. They are goal directed. We select and maintain these concepts and convictions about life. Hence, the perception of reality is developmental in that it continues to build through experience.

An important factor in the formation of the self-concept is the need to belong. Much of the anxiety which influences our personal adjustment is produced because we do not feel we belong; to the extent that we feel inferior, we lack a sense of belonging.

One of the major tasks in personal-social adjustment is the movement from dependency to independence. As the child is guided to become responsible for his actions and recognized for his contributions, his concept of self is enhanced. His views of self may move from: "I am no good," "Nobody likes me," "I can't do it," to "I'm pretty good," "I can do it," "I'll get it done," "I'm pretty good at certain things and not so good at others."

These changed percepts are the result of his experiences and his creative interpretation of experiences. Teachers can actually bring about a change in personal-social adjustment through their relationship with the child. As they act in an encouraging manner, the child's mistaken attitudes and faulty values may be reformulated.

> David was a second grader who took a passive attitude toward his school work. All at once he started to be very disturbing in the room. He would make silly noises and detract from any study that might have been in progress.
> The teacher started out of the room to make some telephone calls in connection with a project that the group was working on. Just as she left the room, David started to make silly noises; he also made some movements which she could detect by the reflection in the window of the door. She turned around, came back quietly, and asked if anyone knew of someone who was through working and could help with two phone calls. One girl suggested David. He looked surprised but went along and looked up a number in the phone book while the teacher made the first call. Since the other phone call was for the same information and he had heard what the teacher asked, she asked David to make the second call for the class, so that she could get back to class.
> When David came back in the room, he started to report to the teacher. She stopped him and asked that he tell the class what he had found out. He reported that the lady had a lamb and some kittens either of which would be tame enough to bring to school for a day.
> David was chosen to be the chairman and selected his committee to make plans for the lamb's visit the following week. He brought wire and made a pen, and one other child brought some hay.
> When the day came for the lamb's visit, all went well until it was time for the class to write a story together about the lamb. The project came to a stop when we discovered that we couldn't give the lamb a name because we didn't know its sex. David offered to phone and find out, which he did.
> When the lamb was taken home after school, David stayed and cleaned up the room. On the way out he said, "Today was such a short day at school I didn't know it was time to go home."

Comment: Here is a child whose purposes were obviously to obtain attention by being disturbing and inadequate. Note that the teacher did not come back to attend to the disturbing action, which would have been exactly what the boy expected. She also accepted the suggestion to have David assist with the phone call. By-passing the opportunity for moralizing, she obviously had an impact upon his evaluation of himself. One can sense the growing development of social interest and cooperation within the child as a result of the teacher's attitude and the changed perception of his place in the group. In achieving improved status, David was able to give up the socially unacceptable behavior.

Late in October, Eddie, a boy who had formerly lived in the neighborhood, returned and was placed in the class. He, I was told by teachers and children, was known to steal (among other problems).

After two or three days one of the children missed some money and burst out, "Eddie stole my money!" At this another child immediately and vehemently cried out, "It can't be! Nothing in this room is ever stolen. It is just misplaced." The second outburst was so intense that it seemed to me to be almost shocking to Eddie. He didn't even defend himself but sat as though stunned and unbelieving. I said nothing but tried to remain calm while work continued.

Later in the day the money was found, and the incident closed inconspicuously. It was my feeling that the confidence the class showed in Eddie had given him a remarkable lift and mark of respect which he had never had in this school. He was thereafter a member of good standing in the group.

Comment: It is clear that Eddie had developed a reputation which was bound to influence his view of self and the world. The atmosphere developed within the room by this teacher was such that not all of the children were immediately willing to point the finger of suspicion at Eddie. The respect shown Eddie by the class gave him a place which he had never before held. The creation of a therapeutic atmosphere in the classroom by teachers is another method to facilitate personal-social adjustment.

As the personality of the child develops, certain convictions about life begin to emerge. These convictions are about himself, and his own values and goals, and about others and how they feel toward him. The child functions on the basis of these convictions regardless of their relationship to reality. It is thus more important to know how a child feels about a situation than to acquire objective evidence about the situation. We can only become aware of the child's convictions and basic purposes by focusing on his perception of reality. If the child feels that he does not belong or that his belonging is dependent upon passive behavior or destructive actions, obviously he will function as though this were fact even though others do not see the situation that way at all.

> Mike was an intelligent boy in the fifth grade who found the mistakes of his classmates very amusing. He laughed at them and was openly contemptuous. He occasionally got into fights at the playground. When he was asked to write an essay about himself he dwelt on the theme that he was a bad boy and could never keep out of trouble, even when he tried. I told him that I didn't agree with him, that neither he nor anyone else was "bad," and that I would try to help him keep out of trouble if he really wanted to be friendly. I said we couldn't allow anyone to laugh at a person who made mistakes because he would be so embarrassed that he could not think clearly. I reminded him of some of the boys who had been friendly to him. I told him that I liked him and was glad to have him in my room in spite of the fact that I sometimes had to ask him to leave the room when he was cruel.
>
> Another boy in the class was having trouble with reading and could not read the social-study book at all. I asked Mike if he would be willing to help him by listening to him read out in the hall and by studying the social-study material with him. Mike seemed to be glad to try this. He did a very good job of it all the rest of the year. He was friendly and patient with Richard, and they became good friends. He never gave up his cruel teasing completely, but it became less frequent. He looked at himself in a less critical light, too.

Comment: Here is an example of a child who felt he was bad and destined to be a troublemaker. Many children assume this attitude, and the very interaction that their behavior inspires in adults seems to fortify the mistaken concepts. Thus the child produces in others the response he expects and increasingly comes to believe that he is inadequate.

It would have been easy for the teacher to follow Mike's lead since his behavior must have been annoying and disruptive to the organization of her group. However, she refused to behave in line with Mike's expectations, although she did do some preaching.

Most important of all, she indicated to him that she liked him and that her acceptance of him was not dependent upon his behaving in some preconceived manner. The acceptance was complete, even though occasionally he might be requested to leave the group. She also found a way for Mike to function within the group and change his position. You will note that she first determined if he would be willing to cooperate and then, assuming that he would behave responsibly, turned the job over to him. As is frequently pointed out, we cannot always expect complete change without additional therapeutic assistance. However, Mike did begin to move in the right direction and certainly this experience initiated a new series of social relationships for him.

> Dick began first grade in my room. At the beginning of the year he appeared to be very noisy, belligerent, and unconcerned about what he did.
>
> One day Dick was doing his writing and making more of a mess than usual when I said to him, "Dick, I know you can do better than that." He replied, "Oh, no, I can't. I can't do anything that is good." I then asked, "Where did you get that idea?" He said, "My brothers and sisters think I'm not good in anything. I always make mistakes. They say everything I do is baby stuff."
>
> Dick was always one of the first children to arrive at school each day. One morning I said to him, "Dick, I need help badly. I am such a forgetful person that I never change the calendar and it is never in order. I have been watching for a good dependable person to be my helper and take care of the calendar. I think you are just that kind of person. Would you like to have that job?" He answered quickly, "I sure would." Then he thought a while and added, "But maybe I will forget, too." I said, "Oh, you can't possibly be as forgetful as I am. But if you should forget that will be okay, too." From then on he was my calendar helper and never made a mistake. I praised him highly for this, and he was very pleased. Because I made quite a bit of his dependability, the other children chose him quite frequently for other room duties which he performed just as well. Then I could praise him more.
>
> I had conferences with his mother, and she helped at home by seeing that the other members of the family encouraged him as well. Each day they let him tell about his school work and his jobs, etc. They took time to listen to what he had to say, and no one was permitted to call it "baby stuff." His mother said he was most proud of being a dependable calendar helper because he did it better than his teacher.
>
> Gradually his school work improved. His belligerence seemed to stop overnight. Best of all, his attitude improved immensely. He truly became one of my best pupils.

Comment: Here was a child whose past experiences had led him to believe that he was not able to function as well as the other members of his family. Hence, he came to school with a belligerent at-

titude. The natural inclination of the teacher might have been to
show Dick who was the boss. Instead, she decided to show him that
he could be of service to her. This again shows the wisdom of giving
jobs and responsibilities to children who need them, and not to
the children who have "earned them." The "good" children do not
need to be rewarded continuously, but *the discouraged children do
need an opportunity to serve.*

Even when Dick indicated his uncertainty about his ability to
perform the task adequately, the teacher assured him that this
would not be a problem.

She took one more step which was most helpful. The parent
conference was used to convey to the mother the need for changing
Dick's position at home. Whenever it is possible to secure home
cooperation, the benefits to the child will obviously be more extensive.

Horizontal vs. Vertical Movement

Many difficulties of adjustment in the personal and social areas
are related to a faulty view of progress and development. Some people tend to think of progress as movement from an inferior to a
superior position. This is putting an emphasis on movement in a
vertical plane. The tendency here is to strive to be on top, to be
more than others. This is frequently achieved by attempting to
bring others down from their previously held superior status.

Healthier movement occurs on a horizontal plane. The individual can express social interest through a concern for mutual progress and goals which do not necessitate his being above others. What
an individual accomplishes is measured from his own point of de-
parture. Progress, then, can be directly related to one's prior position and is not necessarily a function of position within the group.
One can fulfill oneself best by cooperating. The development of
social interest and social equality provides satisfaction.

All of these constructs obviously relate closely to attitudes
developed within the family setting and at school. As adults come
to see for themselves the benefits derived from a noncompetitive atmosphere, they are freed to create this atmosphere for the child.

> Chuck, age eleven, had the notorious reputation of being the
> worst discipline problem in the entire school. When forced to submit
> to authority he rebelled by talking back, being sullen, refusing to
> answer, skipping classes, and failing to complete his school work,

which was below average in the first place. When playing with other children at the playground, he usually got into a fight, and if it was allowed to continue, always won. His constant misbehavior kept him in hot water all the time. A school day never passed without his being lectured, scolded, sent from the room or to the principal's office, or kept after school.

After suspending Chuck for three days the principal confessed that the boy just could not be reached.

I observed Chuck very carefully for several months, never having any direct contact with the boy. One day I sent his teacher a note, asking to see him. When he came into the room, the only response he anticipated from me was a scolding or punishment; to my first question, "Why do you think I sent for you?" he responded that he must have done something wrong. No teacher had ever called him for any other reason.

"No, Chuck," I began, "I called for you because I need a color guard. You are taller and stronger than most other boys here at school; that is why I want you to carry the American flag into the auditorium for the next P.T.A. meeting Tuesday night."

Chuck seemed really glad to accept this position; he took it to heart, never missed a meeting, was always punctual, and looked neat and clean. (This was quite a contrast to his everyday school appearance.) His attitude at school began to change also. Toward the end of the school year when graduating students are preparing to leave our school, I have the "veteran" Junior Safety Patrols train younger members for the next year. Again I especially asked Chuck to join the patrol even though his teacher had not put him on the list of most responsible children. I explained to him that sometimes smaller children got into minor fights while waiting to cross the street and that he would have to stop them. I told him that I could trust him, because he was old enough to know how Patrols should act while on duty.

In response Chuck beamed; it was almost like plugging in the Christmas tree lights. I later learned from the "veteran" patrols that he was using proper procedures in handling the children at the crosswalk, etc., and that there was not one complaint of any misbehavior on his part.

Comment: Chuck "belonged" by being the most rebellious and hostile. His direction was in the vertical plane, trying to outdo others through destructive methods.

It is interesting to note that the principal suspended Chuck. Since the boy already derived little satisfaction from school, we might ask how this action could be expected to correct Chuck's behavior.

The teacher began by showing him that she needed his assistance. His assets were pointed out, and the opportunity to function positively was presented. One observes that Chuck's attitude changed as the opportunity was provided for him to be a success by movement on the horizontal plane. By showing her faith and trust in him, the teacher enabled Chuck to see himself in a new light.

TRAINING AS A SIBLING

Consideration of the child's psychological position in relationship to the sibling is vital when attempting to understand his personal and social adjustment. Each child's position in the family is unique, and he, therefore, can interpret life in his own special manner. One should consider the ordinal position and the expectations classically associated with it. Determining the child's position also demands an examination of the age of each child in the family, the total age spread, the differences in age between the various children, and the distribution of sexes.

The child's position within the family constellation affects his emerging self-concept and life style. The interaction in the sibling relationship produces the training ground for the development of personality traits.

Siblings are aware of their relative positions and the competition which develops among them promotes certain basic personality differences. As they compete, one gives up where the other succeeds and conversely moves in to achieve where the other fails. Competition, therefore, is most significant in the development of personality differences.

Mutality between siblings can be noted in the similarity of traits, temperaments, and interests. These similarities are often based on the common family environment and the lack of any benefit to be accrued from competition.

One must remember that here we are talking about the child's total experience in the sibling relationship and not just the objective events that occur. What occurs is not so significant as what is perceived.

Twins Jill and Joan were in my class. Jill had been quite outspoken and a leader since the beginning of the school year. Joan was the quiet one of the pair. Although she liked to talk and wasn't shy, she always let Jill get ahead and take over. One day I asked Joan if she would like to be the chairman of a group working on a social-studies project. She said that she thought Jill could do a better job, but I told her that with her skill in drawing, she was needed as the chairman in order to help the others. She became the chairman, and Jill was in her group. The project was done beautifully, and Joan learned to lead as her sister learned to follow.

Comment: Joan obviously had given up on herself as a leader. The differences in personality were related to the way she reacted to the competition. Joan lacked the courage that Jill readily exhibited. The teacher took Joan's asset and used it to change her position within the group and in relation to Jill. This was a particularly valuable experience since it permitted both of the children to develop socially and personally.

William, age nine, had an older brother, age twelve, who had a reputation for fighting and for aggression against other children and teachers. He was also known for stealing, poor academic achievement, and truancy. William was viewed generally in the light of his brother's reputation but did not exhibit any of the negative behavior. He was an indifferent student but showed promise in arithmetic. He liked to put his feet on his desk, wear his hair like a floor mop, and keep his finger in his nose. He rarely paid attention but occupied himself by breaking his eraser into small pieces and throwing the pieces at the other children. He also threw spitballs. He stopped immediately if I called his name. I concluded that he wanted the children to notice him. He was neglected at the playground, which also made me think that he wanted attention from the children and status in the class.

One of our units in science was on electricity, and for a change he read his assignment. His father was a skilled machinist, and I wondered if William might have an interest along this line. I walked back to his desk. He sat up in his chair and stopped making spit balls when he saw me. "See what you can work out as an experiment, Bill," I said. "I'll help if you will tell me what you need. Maybe Jim would like to work with you." William's eyes glinted, and Jim looked interested. They had a list of wire, batteries, and doorbell at my desk in a short time. I showed them where to find everything and suggested that they be ready to explain their work to the class.

William did a fine job, quickly and efficiently. The children listened to his explanation and delighted in the ringing doorbell. The next day he came to school with his hair slicked back and his face shining clean. "Can I work with the science kit when I finish my work?" he asked. I gave him permission. His behavior in school changed immediately.

Comment: William evidenced the results of his interpretation of his position in life. His training in the sibling relationship had led him to certain fallacious assumptions. Children who are deeply discouraged and who lack faith in themselves require a carefully planned approach.

This teacher chose not to comment on the negative behavior. She took advantage of his having read the material and of his already developed interest. She arranged to have him work in a situation where he could demonstrate his skills. To be certain that the experience was a success, she helped in providing the material. The important action, though, occurred when she showed her faith to such an extent that William could believe in himself. When we enable the child to change his position, we also enable him to revise his goals, assumptions, and values.

The Teacher and the Staff

Much of the child's personal and social adjustment is acquired through observation. It is important that the teacher and the total staff of the school demonstrate a democratic spirit of cooperation. The relationships among the staff can set the tone for the atmosphere within the building.

The interactions between teachers and children are important in developing adjustment. However, it is equally vital to be aware that the interpersonal behavior of the adults in a particular setting continually sets an example for the children. One cannot decide that this is unimportant in the child's development, because these interactions will affect the mental health of all concerned.

As the teachers take responsibility for facilitating the personal and social adjustment of the pupil, they will note a carryover in effectiveness within the classroom. The teacher who is concerned about the individual is usually able to enlist the support of the class. The total staff must be trained not only to recognize but also to tolerate variability in students. We must accept the child as he is before we can hope to affect his behavior.

Teachers who are concerned about personal and social development will be interested in relaying information to the child's next teacher or to the child's other teacher. This information should be of such a nature that it gives a clear picture of the child's strengths and assets and suggests, perhaps in anecdotal fashion, ways that are effective in working with him. Obviously it should also point clearly to the goals, purposes, and values esteemed by the child.

> When I began my practice teaching in biology in sophomore high school, Joe was one of the first pupils pointed out to me by the teacher as "absolutely no good." Joe's problem and the teacher's was that he refused to participate, even though forced by law to attend school until his sixteenth year. He would not answer questions, study, do homework, or take examinations. Joe was simply sitting out the three months until his sixteenth birthday.
>
> Joe was tall and ungainly in a room full of younger, shorter pupils. There were thirty-eight in the class, and they were packed into the room shoulder to shoulder. For the first three days I observed Joe, and at the end of that time I put at Joe's shoulder a very pretty little blond girl (Sandy) of model deportment, whom I had seen Joe admiring in an unguarded moment. The next step was to give Joe an opportunity to perform. I felt that if I could involve him once, the game would be half won; so I asked for the tallest boy in the room to get a chart down from a ceiling rack, knowing that Joe's 6' 1" dwarfed everyone else in the room. When he hesitated, I thought the game was lost, but he finally arose and pulled down the chart.
>
> When Sandy was excited over a piece of fur, Joe immediately showed interest in furs. I taught him to skin little animals and assigned as his project the trapping of mice, to note kinds, fur types and colors, etc. Next he became very interested in the insects which harmed his "fur" collection and began to study life cycles and habits of insects. One thing led to another. Joe made up his high-school work and went on to college and medical school. I have never heard whether he finished, how he did, or what kind of doctor he made. However, I do know that his attitude toward school had changed.

Comment: The information that had been passed on about Joe obviously could not be of assistance to the new teacher, who used her knowledge of the group and Joe to bring about change. In selecting something that he could do for her she found an area in which she could win him over. She also used his interests to develop new skills. Joe is probably a good example of a child who went through school being considered "impossible" and as a result lived up to his reputation. As teachers learn to communicate more effectively, observe more keenly, and understand purposes, this type of student will turn up less frequently.

When we seek to change the child's personal-social behavior, we must begin by showing our faith in his value as a person. Our belief in him enables him to develop faith in his own ability. We can also make use of the group for enhancing development of the individual.

Changes in the personal-social area produce better adjusted and more effective children with the concomitant development of skills related to the educational process.

Encouragement Techniques
Adapted to
seven | # Developmental Levels

Encouragment implies acceptance of the individual as he is. It is facilitated when we see things as the child sees them and when we recognize the child's creative power to interpret.

It is important to recognize certain developmental differences in children. These developmental differences are a result of the interaction of hereditary endowment, environmental influence, and the child's concept of life, his life style. Although the general principles of encouragement are applicable at any age level, it is valuable to see the child in the context of his specific developmental setting. The very young child obviously is not able to function as effectively in certain areas as the more mature child. He is limited by his physical equipment and his background of experiences. The young child is still actively engaged in trying to find his place and establish his image of self. His life style is still in the process of development. His approach to the life tasks is still being formulated.

As the child matures he comes into conflict with authority. His parents and teachers have more of a problem controlling his behavior and thus become cognizant of the need to manage behavior effectively.

It is most important that a good relationship be established with the child from the start. The effectiveness of your efforts with the child is based on his acceptance of you and your values.

The style of life is in the process of formation early in life. Many basic concepts and convictions can be changed with relative ease when compared with the difficulty in changing personality later in life.

Those who deal with the primary child, parent and teacher, have much more flexible material to work with in terms of change. After puberty the life style is well established, and change is much more difficult to accomplish.

On the issue of changes in goals and purposes it is significant to observe that the young child will more readily recognize his goals and give up certain kinds of behavior. With the development of intelligence and rationalizing skills, the recognition of goals and the changing of behavior become increasingly difficult.

We shall not attempt to develop specific characteristics of the various phases of childhood. However, it would be advantageous for us to see the child in the setting of developmental tasks. Havighurst has defined the developmental task as follows:[1]

> A developmental task is a task which arises at or about a certain period in the life of the individual, successful achievement of which leads to his happiness and to success with later tasks, while failure leads to unhappiness in the individual, disapproval by society and difficulty with later tasks.

This concept is useful to us in that it permits us to see the stream of development and assists in our timing of educational efforts. Cognizance of the developmental tasks helps us to recognize goals and purposes as they appear at the various developmental levels. Havighurst has listed the following developmental tasks for two periods of life:[2]

Developmental Tasks of Infancy and Early Childhood

1. Learning to walk
2. Learning to take solid food
3. Learning to talk
4. Learning to control the elimination of the body wastes
5. Learning sex differences and sexual modesty
6. Achieving physiological stability
7. Forming simple concepts of social and physical reality

8. Learning to relate oneself emotionally to parents, siblings, and other people.
9. Learning to distinguish right and wrong and developing a conscience.

Developmental Tasks of Middle Childhood

1. Learning physical skills necessary for ordinary games
2. Building wholesome attitudes towards oneself as a growing organism
3. Learning to get along with age-mates
4. Learning an appropriate masculine or feminine social role
5. Developing fundamental skills in reading, writing, and calculating
6. Developing concepts necessary for everyday living
7. Developing conscience, morality, and a scale of values
8. Achieving personal independence
9. Developing attitudes towards social groups and institutions

As we look at these tasks we come to a better understanding of the child's emerging pattern of behavior. Recognition of the tasks enables us to function within a developmental framework.

The developmental levels we shall discuss are divided as follows: primary grades, intermediate grades, and junior high school. There is always an overlap of developmental groups in any arbitrary division, and the division selected merely permits us to give examples related to specific settings.

Primary Grades

Children in the primary grades are still in the process of formulating many of their concepts relative to school, achievement, and discipline. Encouragement at this level is particularly important in that it plays such an important part in the correction of earlier misconceptions affecting the development of the life styles. For the most part evaluations and interpretations relevant to work tasks and school social life are developed at this time.

Discouragement in the primary child can bring about feelings of inferiority and inadequacy. Progress in school is based on confidence in self. Teachers at this level particularly need to pace material so that it fits appropriate developmental patterns. There is a need to be aware of the child's rate of growth and psychological needs.

Billy was smaller than the other children and immature in many ways. He had been subject to epileptic seizures until he was four years old. Billy was very happy in our first-grade class and disliked being away Saturday and Sunday. He made an effort to do the work presented to him, but he often needed help. He displayed little skill in the academic work.

One day Billy brought a book from our library table and asked if he could take it home. This wasn't one of the books we ordinarily sent home, and it certainly wasn't a book I would have selected for Billy to read. However, I allowed him to take it home.

In a few days he returned the book, read some of it for me, and was most pleased with his progress. This helped Billy gain self-confidence and really improved his work.

Comment: Billy was immature and had a physical handicap. In many ways the teacher could have been discouraged with his progress. However, Billy believed in himself, and the teacher's faith permitted him to succeed. Here we see the efficacy of self-selection and the validity of the simple encouragement implicit in not deciding that the child cannot accomplish something but permitting him to try—the nurture of encouragement.

Encouragement occurs in subtle fashion at times. It is well for the teacher to recognize that she has continual interaction with the child, some of which is encouraging and some discouraging. Her emphasis should be on creating and developing as many opportunities for encouragement as possible. The following incident illustrates how in a simple interaction with the child the teacher could have been punitive but instead recognized the part of the response that was correct and built on that. As we evaluate child responses we need to be aware of the number of things they do correctly and build from there. Instead of pointing out the mistake, being critical, or reprimanding, this teacher stimulated.

The first-grade class was requested to call out words beginning with "S" so that the teacher could list them on the board. Carol, in a moment of forgetfulness, called out the word "city," which begins with an "S" sound but isn't spelled with an "S." The teacher looked thoughtful for a moment and then explained the "C-S" sound confusion. She told the child she was "thinking ahead" and suggested that Carol make up a list of words from day to day that started with "C" and sounded like "S" and then present the list to the other children. This encouraged the child's interest in words and spelling, and she went on to become one of the best spellers in her school and town.

•

Sometimes children feel incapable of meeting the expectations of adults. The tasks appear to be much larger than anything they can accomplish. Here we need to facilitate readiness by building on present skills and strengths. The story of Robert will show a teacher who moved a child from a minus to a plus situation by recognizing what he could do and starting there.

Robert was smaller in size than his third-grade peers and experienced difficulty in learning how to write, although his printing was excellent. When he saw the progress that other pupils were making, he became discouraged and preferred to print his assignments.

By telling Robert that his printing was of excellent quality and by reasoning with him that his writing could be as beautiful if he practiced it for as long a time as he had practiced printing, I encouraged him to attempt writing with a more positive attitude. His writing improved considerably, and he was further encouraged when I showed his writing to the class by displaying his papers and by having him write announcements on the blackboard.

Comment: Often it is important to involve the child completely in the class to get his best effort. Encouragement is applied by finding the child's assets, or interests, and involving him first on his terms. Sometimes children do not function well in an area because they lack courage to begin.

Philip had entered the first grade late in the school year; he was excellent in reading and other academic subjects but was shy and rather poorly coordinated in his large muscles. He did not enjoy running games in gym, throwing a ball, and so forth, and during free play would frequently come to the classroom teacher and the physical-education teacher to talk.

One day the physical-education teacher distributed scarves among the children and told them they were to do anything they wanted with them while music was playing on the record player. This appealed to the artistic sensitivity of the shy boy. He improvised an interesting routine which looked like a butterfly. The teacher stopped the music and asked all the children to sit in a circle. She mentioned what interesting things they were all doing with their scarves and referred to Philip's routine. She then told them all to get up once more. Of course, many eyes were on Philip; yet he did not feel that he was having to perform alone and beamed as he elaborated his routine.

After the scarves were turned in the teacher said, "Philip has been showing us such good ideas this morning that I would like to hear what game he would like us to play and have him start it." Philip beamed and chose "Fire Engine" in which he began as caller. At the end of the period Philip went to the gym teacher and said, "Gym was fun today, Miss R."

Comment: The teacher grasped the opportunity to note something praiseworthy that the child was doing. She seized the opportunity to build on his asset. Attitudes and values can be changed readily when one encourages and facilitates a change in the child's position in the group.

> Richard was often a disturbing influence in the classroom by talking to his neighbors, making wisecracks, etc. During art class he looked at everyone else's accomplishments before he began. He often drew a good picture but at the last minute would give all the men in the picture long cigarettes or all the people measles, etc. Everyone around him would look at his picture and laugh.
>
> One day after we had discussed a movie we had just seen, we proceeded to draw pictures. The movie was about land and water. Richard drew a beautiful picture of a boat sailing on a lake, with snow-capped mountains in the distance. I thought it was exceptionally well done, and after telling him so, I asked if he wanted to pin it up on the back board. Richard was in his glory. In every art class thereafter Richard used every medium that was presented in a picture of snow-capped mountains and sailboats on a lake.

Comment: Richard originally found his place by being the clown. The teacher needed to move him to a constructive pattern. Spotting the opportunity in a well-done drawing, she enabled Richard to experience success. In a sense teachers can arrange success experiences. This is an example of manipulation to benefit the child. The next step would be to let him see the acceptability of a variety of ideas in his work.

Intermediate Grades

The child who enters the intermediate grades is generally in an accelerated period of growth. This is the preadolescent growth cycle. There is an increased desire on the part of the child for self-direction.

The teacher at this level will find encouragement a real asset in bringing about desirable behavior and personality development. Encouragement can also enhance the learning situation.

Here is another example of the teacher's ability to influence the child's feelings of adequacy, security, and self-confidence.

Danny had been performing inadequately in school. He seldom found things he could do well. After returning from a short illness, Danny found himself the head of the bulletin-board committee. As soon as he heard the news he came up to me and said, "I'm not sure I can do it, Mrs. S." I asked him what were the three things necessary for a good bulletin board. He said, "Interest, good ideas, and a working committee." We went through each of these, and I finished by saying that I was *sure* he could do a good job.

The subject he chose was stock-car racing, whether or not it was a sport. The board went up, and he was justifiably proud. Even in the critical evaluation by the students he did well. Most important was his look of satisfaction as the boys flipped through the many books he had on display and then came to him for further information.

Comment: Danny lacked belief in himself and in his ability to produce. The teacher in simple fashion indicated the essentials necessary for the job and expressed her complete confidence in his ability. Through this demonstration of faith Danny's position in the classroom was enhanced. This illustrates well that encouragement can be a very simple process, but one which accomplishes much for the child's development.

Mary was afraid to speak in front of her class and was extremely shy. At home she had been made to feel inadequate and was never allowed to express herself without being laughed at or criticized by members of the family. Her teacher began to praise her when she spoke a few words, and soon confidence in herself was built up. She began to feel less inferior and to feel that she had some individual worth. She needed attention and understanding, and as she received them she was able to give of herself in situations where she had before felt inadequate.

Comment: Teachers will find that the child is a product of many experiences in the home, community, and family before he arrives in their classrooms. Mary's teacher was aware of her feelings of inadequacy. She built on the little bit that Mary was able to produce. The teacher's concept of Mary facilitated the change in some of Mary's basic assumptions about life and herself.

Encouragement requires the teacher to disregard past negative information she may have received. Children frequently come to class with an established record of failure. Some of these children have experienced certain gains by convincing the teacher that they cannot function. The child in the intermediate grades who has convinced the teacher that he cannot read is often excused from a number of the work tasks at school. Frequently he is thereby set free to concentrate on nuisance activities. We shall now see the type of child who the teacher is likely to feel is impossible to help.

> I had given up. Archie was a nonreader. He came into the fifth grade not reading, and it looked as if he was going to leave the same way.
> It was late in the winter. The girls and boys were discussing their science projects. One of the children wanted to demonstrate the working of a doorbell. He had all the materials for his demonstration, but he could not get the doorbell to work.
> Archie said, "Mrs. J, let me try, let me try." I said, "Go ahead, Archie. Here are the directions in your science text," and I gave him the book knowing that he could not read.
> Believe it or not, he had the bell working in a reasonable number of minutes. I asked him to tell the class how he did it. His face lighted up like a Christmas tree.
> I could have told Archie, "No, you can't read the directions in your text." Instead, I gave him the book as if I expected him to read. He gave the book to another pupil to read to him. I chose to ignore that fact and praised him for what he had done.
> At the close of the day, I asked Archie to remain after school. I invited him to look through the books on electricity which I had brought from the library to see if there were anything in them he would like to try. He selected Zim's *Things around the House*. I asked him to take the book home, study the diagrams, find out what we would need to work with, and whether or not we had the materials.
> The next day when he returned I asked, "How did you come out, Archie?" He looked at me rather sheepishly and said, "Well, some of these words I don't know." The small words he knew; some I told him; others we worked out together. For the first time, I felt that the printed pages had meaning for Archie.

Comment: This teacher was only functioning in the same manner as many of her colleagues before her. Archie had arrived in Mrs. J's class a failure in reading and had convinced her that reading was beyond him. The busy teacher frequently focuses on children who appear to benefit from her guidance. Archie was too discouraged to cope with. The roles of student and teacher were well-established, and little progress was expected from either.

Observe closely how Mrs. J seized upon the opportunity for a positive contribution. When Archie asked to try she did not say that they did not have time to waste but patiently permitted him to proceed. She was not going to pass up a chance when Archie was willing. For the moment her traditional expectations were dropped as she permitted him to function. Admittedly she was amazed. She should not have been, however, because frequently children can perform in certain areas beyond their verbal capacities. However, school does not always provide the opportunities for such a demonstration.

This teacher also was not willing to let the episode pass as an incidental success. She spent time attempting to select the next most appropriate experience from her available materials. Although the book selected was beyond the child, he did make the attempt and movement was begun.

In a similar instance one might use the experience-story approach and have the child develop and dictate his story to you. It has been demonstrated repeatedly that the size of words is insignificant in the development of a reading vocabulary. Children can read their own stories at a rather high level of comprehension.

The above incident provided us with a specific situation in which a child came to change. Sometimes we cannot identify so readily the factors that bring change.

> Dick had not done much work in school up to the fifth grade. His parents were at their wits' end. He was not interested in doing anything. He would come home from school, put on his pajamas, and go to bed.
>
> His fifth-grade teacher, a man, was aware of this history and proceeded by expecting him to get his work done on time and by treating him like all the other students. He acted as if he felt Dick would perform. Dick began to pick up in his work, made friends, and was accepted by the class. Much progress was made during the fifth grade.

Comment: This teacher was not convinced by Dick's previous record of failure. He believed that if Dick were treated as though he was expected to function he would function. The teacher refused to let Dick be something special, and Dick soon began to belong on the teacher's terms.

This will not work with all children. The subtle factor in this incident was the general atmosphere and the teacher's philosophy. This teacher gets to know each child well. When he is convinced that there is no structural reason for ineffective learning, he proceeds as if he were certain the child would produce.

The creative teacher is not limited by traditional approaches to learners with problems. She is not concerned with her status but instead earnestly seeks something that works.

> Peter, product of a bilingual home, had a language difficulty. He was learning to read, but at a very slow rate. One day after school when he stayed to help me, I asked if he could teach me some Spanish. He was thrilled. He went home and told his family all about it. I had some Spanish background, and we began to teach each other. He was teaching me his language; I was helping him in reading.

Comment: This teacher found an asset in Peter, his Spanish ability. She showed a genuine interest in learning from the child. This developed a reciprocally helpful relationship. It also permitted Peter to recognize that even teachers can have problems in learning. Certainly his concept of his status in relationship to the teacher had to change.

One of the most important functions of the teacher is to develop a sound knowledge of each child's assets. Typically, the teacher is better able to diagnose each child's weaknesses. However, when we come to see a child's strengths, we can build a new relationship. The story of Bill shows how a teacher stumbled into this success. Some time devoted to an interest inventory and to a brief interview with each child can assist in making the following incident typical rather than atypical.

> Bill was much larger than the average boy in his fourth-grade class. He was constantly touching and bothering his classmates and as a result was unpopular. He had been tested frequently, and it was determined that his I.Q. was quite high. He was also found to have exceptional talents in music. Although he had the capacity to do very well in school work, his work was always sloppy and below average. He was interested only in writing music.
>
> Early in the year the class became interested in the various countries of the world, and Bill volunteered to investigate the music of each. His interest soon led him to bring some extremely interesting material to class. The group wanted to share their materials with other classes. In order to present the materials they had to be organized in a presentable fashion. This required class time. Soon Bill was getting all work in acceptably so that he would have time to work on the project.

Comment: Bill, like many children, had not found his place. Thus, his general talents were not permitted to function. Once the opportunity was presented to show to advantage in the general setting, he became able to function in a number of areas.

Although it is not always possible to incorporate each child's interests into the classroom, we should be aware that learning proceeds much more readily when the material is personally significant and the child can truly become involved.

> Cathy comes from an intellectually deprived home environment. There are seven children and Cathy's father is unknown. Records showed average mental ability, and Cathy entered fourth grade at nine years of age.
>
> Of all the subjects taught, arithmetic was the only one where she showed lack of confidence. Her third-grade teacher had also indicated some "block" in this area and reported frequent pouting over assignments.
>
> One day, following dismissal, I asked Cathy to remain briefly for some "experimenting" with the chalk board. She seemed to enjoy the work and especially appreciated praise for accuracy. Because there was evidence of a great need for approval, I watched her work daily and was quick to point out her continued accuracy and improvement. She was particularly pleased when assigned to help another classmate who was in need of extra practice. Cathy gradually grew confident and for the remainder of the year approached new work in arithmetic without hesitation, and the quality of her work matched her performance in other areas.

Comment: Sometimes a small amount of time devoted to the individual child can reap benefits impossible to achieve through mass instructional approaches. Cathy responded well to genuine praise. However, the teacher recognized that the approach had to be consistent and followed through on her daily work. When Cathy had progressed to the point where she could be recognized for her efforts, the teacher used her to help another child. This placed added value on Cathy and illustrates how two children can facilitate each other's development.

Junior High School

The junior-high-school child may be particularly hard to live with and understand. His behavior, sometimes boisterous, sometimes antagonistic, can be most disconcerting to the adult. He is in

between in that he is no longer a baby but in our society is certainly
not a grownup.

There is an ever increasing conflict between peer and adult demands, and it is difficult to maintain equilibrium between them.
His relationship to the group is now a more vital concern than it
had been previously. The conflict with parental desires now moves
toward a peak. He may even reject parental guidance. This behavior, usually occurring either at the beginning or at the end of a
developmental period, is known to be more deviant than behavior
which occurs during periods of rapid development.

The child now aspires to greater independence and often places
an exaggerated emphasis on the need to be independent. More than
ever he is anxious to participate in decisions and problems involving the family.

Peer sex roles are also of primary consideration. Boys are concerned about living up to boy requirements, and girls seek one another's approval. The child matures when he finds a friend whose
importance to him equals or even exceeds his own self-importance.

In the next example a referral to the principal's office presents
the opportunity to correct the child's faulty assumption. The boy is
shown his worth instead of subjected to preaching and punishing.

Roger, a big seventh-grade boy reading at third-grade level, was
sent to the principal for making loud remarks in science class. The
dialogue follows:

Mrs. R: Why, I thought you liked science.
Roger: I did when we had electricity, but this stuff, I can't even read
        the words.
Mrs. R: You could listen and learn something about how that fine
        body of yours works.
Roger: It's Mrs. G. She hates me. If she hears a noise, she kicks me
        out.
Mrs. R: You are quiet, but Mrs. G blames you when others mis-
        behave?
Roger: Well, no, not always. I guess I'm just no good. Teachers hate
        kids that can't do anything.
Mrs. R: Who changed the bulb in Mrs. C's projector when no one
        else could?
Roger: That was easy.
Mrs. R: Who found the loose wire in the P.A. machine when the
        eighth grade couldn't make it work?
Roger: That was just luck. I wiggled it, and it made a noise.

Mrs. R: Well, it's the kind of luck we need around here, and you seem to have it. It isn't luck, Roger, it is mechanical ability, and the world needs a lot of it. Now show me what you were having this science period, and I'll show you how you can surprise Mrs. G with a drawing of it when the period is over.

Roger made a drawing of the circulatory system on which Mrs. G complimented him at the end of the period. His work in this class progressively improved as teacher and child focused on assets.

Comment: Roger felt inferior, and his behavior in class only produced difficulty. He was identifying the teacher as his source of difficulty and hence was most uncooperative. It is interesting to note that the principal did not go on the attack but stopped to listen. She established an atmosphere of mutual respect. Next she took the time to specify the good things that Roger had done; she placed value on Roger. Even though he was so discouraged with himself that he could not take credit for his achievements, she produced several examples which illustrated that Roger could function effectively. Finally, she made use of Roger's abilities so that he could also function effectively in this situation. Children can be changed when we set out to facilitate success through encouragement.

Larry, age thirteen, in the eighth grade, dreaded social-studies committee work because of his difficulty in reading eighth-grade content materials. When the class began a unit on the United Nations, he begged not to be put on a committee because he would be embarrassed and felt he could contribute nothing.

I knew, however, that he had been interested in the construction projects that had been mentioned in discussing the activities of UNESCO, UNICEF, etc. and that he enjoyed art activities. I found several books at fifth- and sixth-grade reading level which discussed and described the work done by children of various countries in connection with these activities and got him started on panoramas depicting the projects. I also expressed my belief that he would be making a useful contribution to the class because I knew how well he would carry out the project.

Larry's success in this project not only restored his self-confidence and gained him recognition from the group but increased his confidence in his ability to improve in reading.

Comment: Larry's ability to identify with his group adequately was hampered by lack of certain school skills. He felt that he could not contribute and hence could not belong. Again the teacher took the first step when she identified his strengths, assets, and interests. She also provided materials that were at his level and were paced to permit success. Then she involved him in a project that was success oriented. She did not hesitate to express her faith in Larry. We see a change in skills and position in the group developing from this opportunity to be a success. Larry was now free to function and believe in himself.

> Kenneth, thirteen years old, needed some extra help in understanding and working with percentages. My first special session with him wasn't too pleasant because he was so uncooperative. Several days later he asked me questions about using an air-speed and altitude computer. He was very interested in learning how to fly a plane and read technical books on the subject. This interest of his gave me an idea. Since his difficulty in working with percentages seemed to be greater when working with word problems, I rewrote some of the problems using air speeds and altitudes of planes and, in the process, used some aspects of working with the computer. He showed more enthusiasm during our second work period, and we worked together much longer than I had expected. He was doing a good job, and I praised his work. Although my problems did not have as practical an application as those in the book, we did make progress in understanding percentages.

Comment: This incident gives us some insight into proper remedial procedures. Of course, Kenneth was uncooperative at the start; he had been convinced that this was his role and his place. This teacher, too, began by investigating his interests. She then adapted the work. This indicated Kenneth's value and her faith in him. Recognition now could genuinely be given for Kenneth's efforts. It is interesting to note that even though the approach was eminently successful, the teacher questioned its value compared to that of the book. This teacher, too, could benefit by being encouraged to have faith in her approach to children.

> In a unit study of geography, part of the lesson required learning the states and their capitals. At the conclusion of the unit I gave a matching test of capitals and states. Gerry, whose apparent interest in the whole unit was very low, failed the test and came up to my desk with his paper and the remark, "I think this is real silly stuff anyway." I let the remark go unanswered.
> Several days later during an art period I suggested that perhaps the class would like to draw maps of our country and outline the states. I noticed while Gerry was working on his map he also was

studying a page in his geography book. When his map was finished, he brought it up to my desk. I said, "How very nice, Gerry. I can see you have worked very hard on this." Two days later he stopped me after school and said, "I sure had fun doing that map. Name any state and I will tell you the capital." And he did!

Comment: Gerry showed open resistance to this part of learning. He deliberately challenged the teacher. It is interesting to note that the teacher refused to respond by demanding or being more powerful. Instead, she permitted Gerry to work on the problem at his own pace. The atmosphere was such that Gerry still had the problem, not the teacher. She recognized his efforts and built a new relationship. The results were obviously of a nature that she could never have produced through force and pressure.

Footnotes

1 Robert J. Havighurst, *Human Development and Education* (New York: Longmans, Green and Company, 1953), p. 2. Courtesy of David McKay Company, Inc.

2 Havighurst, *Human Development.*

eight | *Encouragement in the Classroom— the Group*

To this point our focus has been on the relationship between the adult and the child. However, all of our assumptions have placed a great emphasis on the importance of the individual's position in the group.

The social meaning of behavior, the importance of considering behavior in terms of its total environment, and the significance of belonging as a basic need, all lead us to a consideration of the role of the group in motivation and encouragement.

The Role of the Group in Encouragement

Children live, grow, develop, and adjust in the group. The child's first group is the family constellation. Here many of his assumptions about life are first developed and tried out. Here he learns his specific role within the family and develops skills in interpersonal relationships.

While the family and the family constellation have always been important in the development of the child, our social climate gives the peer group much greater influence than it has ever exerted before. As we move toward democracy and away from autocracy, the child's peers become increasingly significant to him. We need only to observe the child at free play to note his dependence on peer approval; Usually it is

103

more important than approval by the teacher. The child is frequently much more concerned about accommodating himself to the wishes and directions of his peers than to the rules of the family.

The child will often be restrained or moved by a concern for his position in the group. He is frequently willing to take directions from his peers that he would not accept as readily from adults. This group pressure, then, exists within childhood society. The effective educator will attempt to mobilize group pressure to serve generally acceptable purposes.

One of the primary skills of the educator is the stimulation of proper values in each child. Values are more readily accepted when they provide a feeling of belonging to the group. Thus, the group can become an agent for change and for cooperation.

Each group has its own group personality. One can notice, among other ways in which the group reveals its personality, whether the group is for the teacher or against the teacher, defiant or pleasant, desirous of being educated or opposed to education, divided into cliques or well-integrated.

Rather than let things occur haphazardly, the leader can plan so that the group will stimulate the social adjustment of the child. We are certain that the group has a significant effect upon the development of each child. The teacher's choice lies in whether she wants the influence of the group to occur in a socially acceptable direction, or at random as the spirit of the group may develop.

Group Goals and Objectives

For purposes of discussion, group goals can be divided into constructive and destructive goals. Many of the most difficult children in school are difficult because their goals are centered on destructive objectives. They have switched to socially unacceptable behavior. Their concern for others is low, and their primary identification is with others who also are in opposition.

Confronted with a group whose objectives are basically antisocial, one needs to be clear in the identification of group objectives and in the determination of the purposes of this group behavior.

Group objectives might well center around the development of cooperation. The most effective teachers are quick to sense the need that each child has to find an acceptable place within his group. They frequently take advantage of this need by providing children with jobs which permit them to cooperate in the functioning of the classroom.

Social interest can also be developed in the group. There are many opportunities to show concern for others and to participate in the give and take of human relations. When one realizes the relationship of social interest to mental health, one must be concerned with its development.

Each group consists of a variety of interpersonal relationships. Many of our studies show that the major reason for not succeeding on a job is incapacity to adjust to the group, not lack of job skills. Social adjustment can be taught best within the context of group activities.

Self-understanding is another objective which can come to fruition in the group. One's basic understanding of self always develops partially out of the feedback that one gets from social relationships.

Each group should strive to work at the solving of common tasks. These tasks should be selected by the group and should procide adequate opportunity for all the children to develop responsibility.

Thus, we see that this type of group organization encourages the leaders to set specific goals and objectives. Working within the framework of an understanding of man and his development within society, the leader recognizes the need for developing group goals.

The Teacher as Group Leader

A considerable part of teacher education directs the teacher toward consideration of individual differences. This, at times, causes the teacher to forget that she deals not only with a set number of individuals but with an entire group as well. The teacher must either utilize the group to her advantage, or she will soon find it an obstacle to progress. It is natural that at the beginning the children will have a much greater commitment to the other children than to the teacher. This can be utilized to the advantage of the teacher if she is aware of the children's commitment.

The teacher must become well-acquainted with the forces operating within the group. It is important to understand the dynamics of the individual child, but this must be supplemented with a knowledge of the way in which groups work. The leader needs to understand how the group and its structure change as a result of

internal and external forces. This necessitates an awareness of the
many subgroups which exist within the classroom. Actions which
are disturbing to the teacher are often better understood when
viewed in terms of the interrelationships of the groups. Some children are disturbing because of the recognition that it brings them
from the entire group or from a subgroup with which they feel
affiliated. Other children are completely discouraged in their functioning because they do not feel that they can belong anywhere and
cannot see any opportunity to establish themselves with their peers.

Thus, the teacher who is unaware of existing intergroup relationships cannot be effective in influencing the group. She may acci-
dentally accentuate certain problems because she does not know the
characteristics of the subgroup structure. A knowledge of the group
can assist her in rearranging the structure to facilitate her influence
on both the individual and the entire class. Once the teacher is
alert to interaction within the class, the class can be of great assistance in accomplishing educational goals. Without this knowledge, it
can resist progress.

If the teacher refuses to deal with the group relationships in
order to press toward educational goals, she may permit the disturbing child to get the class cooperating with him instead of with the
teacher. We have all noted instances when the class seemed to be
working at cross-purposes with the teacher. Knowledge of the specific dynamics of a particular group can prevent this from being a
common occurrence.

The children within the class can often be of assistance to one
another once the proper social atmosphere is developed. Without
it, one can observe the negative effect of competition within the
group. It is regularly reported that the major difficulty causing
teachers to be released or to retire from the profession involves
their handling of disciplinary matters. These deficiencies are often
directly related to ineffective handling of group discipline.

The teacher needs to emphasize the communality of classroom
problems. As students are led to see the benefits derived from effective interpersonal relationships, they become more interested in working together. Effective classroom organization calls for the handling
of problems so as to permit the group to work together on their
solution. The problem-solving process will then permit the children

to focus on something that they are mutually involved in and that also meets their need to belong.

The group process calls for a leader who has the ability to make the group aware of what it is doing. This is done in order to produce feedback. It should be brought to the children's attention when they act in a manner disadvantageous to the general development of the group. The purpose of the behavior should be pointed out and opportunities presented to develop more adequate solutions.

Working effectively with a group is a stimulating task. The leader offers encouragement to the group and to its individual members. Through his encouragement the group develops more effective communication. Once communication is established, the children can be focused on solving tasks that involve common interests and concerns.

One can usually find within any class those who are working against the generally accepted purposes. The development of adequate communication among group members usually facilitates attachment to the group goal. Teachers should recognize the need to experiment with new methods and apply them in determining that the opinion being expressed is truly representative of the group.

Although the development of group cohesiveness never proceeds smoothly in the beginning, it is important to focus on integrating all the children into a cohesive classroom group. When this is not done, hostile interests within the group tend to become highly cohesive as Cunningham has pointed out.[1] It would seem, then, that children who are antagonistic to the educational process may often have an ability superior to the teacher's to create group cohesiveness, which they subsequently direct against the teacher.

The teacher, therefore, has a responsibility to use the group to assist in the development of all the children. Many educational disabilities really result from being out of tune with the group and hitting upon ineffective ways to establish a place in the group. Once teachers become sensitive to the interrelationships, they can use them to the benefit of all concerned.

> Susie, a seven-year-old second grader, was one of several Negro children in our integrated school. She had a quick sense of humor and above average intelligence which was manifested primarily in her reading ability. However, she was from a very low-income family and

her appearance (i.e., mode of dress) made her the object of constant ridicule and name calling by two of the white children to the point where she gradually retreated entirely from group participation.

I was aware that the white children also had a problem, but my first concern was with Susie. I found an opportunity to tell the girl how much some of the children missed her humor and comments in class, and in order to help her regain a place in the group, I made Susie storyteller for several days, allowing her to read the books the children brought from home. At this the class realized how much they *had* missed her contributions and almost seemed to organize to draw her back into the group. Susie regained her self-confidence and returned to being her active, cheerful self.

Comment: The observant teacher can frequently note when relationships within the group are strained. This teacher had found a child who was withdrawing completely from the group. Assessing the child, she selected one asset to help her regain her place within the group. This caused the class to recognize Susie's contributions to the group. A simple maneuver thus helped Susie gain significance within the classroom.

Dick, a third grader, was a poor reader. He had been having trouble concentrating on the words and therefore stumbled along quite slowly. I knew that his slowness was due to his lack of concentration. One day I asked Dick if he would please take charge of the slow reading group and try to listen and help the others. I found that this method helped him keep his mind on the words and the idea of the story. From then on he began to improve steadily as his sense of helpfulness and leadership came forward with a little encouragement.

Comment: This teacher did the unexpected in terms of usual teacher behavior. She took a child who was not functioning and gave him responsibility. She implied faith in him by asking that he assist others. Thus, the group became an agent to bring about change in this child. Too often we expect the child to function before we permit him to serve. This teacher reversed the process to the great benefit of the child.

Ronald reached fifth grade long after his reputation, which had preceded him into every classroom since his second year in first grade. His I.Q. was reported to be 75, and he had been treated for petit mal while he was in third grade. His teachers had given up trying to teach him to read or to learn the basic facts of numbers. He had improved in health and was no longer taking medicine, but he was extremely discouraged and cried at every disappointment or reproof. He knew how to subtract simple numbers; so I saw to it that he was given a chance to do a subtraction problem every day on the board. He enjoyed this but would not try to learn other skills. I showed him some pages in a book where all the basic facts of addition, subtraction, multiplication, and division were given without answers. I helped him with these, one row at a time, until he knew them all, forward, backward, and all mixed up. Soon he could do all the addition facts without error in four minutes, the requirement for fifth grade. He was pleased, and the class was very proud of him. Opportunities for him to assist others were soon available.

After much more work he could pass the requirement for the other three operations. By the end of the year he could do long division with two-figure divisors, multiplication with three-figure multipliers, and addition with carrying. All this was accomplished not only because of my encouragement but also that of his classmates.

Comment: Ronald found a new position in the group because he was able to function. Sometimes children establish their place by virtue of what they cannot do. This, then, becomes their role, and their behavior is based on the expectations of the teacher and the group. Because this teacher refused to believe Ronald was ineffective he was permitted to establish a new role. The group helped him develop strength.

Sociometry

We have established that the teacher can play an important role by managing the relationships within the group. In order to do this effectively, though, she needs to have accurate information about relationships within the group. Sociometry was developed by J. L. Moreno to give a picture of specific group structures. It is possible to sense relationships among students, but sociometry provides us with a more accurate picture of the individual child's position in relation to other children. Sociometry provides us with insight into the characteristics of group members and the roles that they play in relationship to one another.

Sociometric data are obtained by asking the individuals to choose other members of the group as companions for specific activities. The proposed activities should arise out of regular classroom activities and might involve having the children choose persons to sit near them, work with them, join them in class projects, or play with them. The technique obviously works most effectively when the atmosphere of the classroom customarily permits choice.

After administration of the sociometric test, children should have the opportunity to carry out their choices. The results are used confidentially in a variety of ways to enable teachers to work with individuals and the group more effectively. It enables the teacher to locate the most frequently chosen children and those who are isolated from the group and the subgroups that exist.

A number of books have been published which supply specific information on the use and collection of sociometric data; some which might be consulted include Gronlund, Jennings, and Moreno.[2] Jennings stresses the importance of long sociometric chains to bring about class integration. The use of sociometric data assists the teacher in diagnosing the structure of the group and enables her to develop corrective efforts, when necessary, to change the nature of the group and subgroups. It frequently helps to spotlight negative forces within the class. It may enable the teacher to separate leaders who are in opposition to the objectives of the educational setting. Of course, it also permits the identification of the cooperative elements within the class. Thus, an opportunity is furnished to integrate isolated children with cooperative groups.

If the teacher is aware of children who are rejected and at the same time is aware of their choices, she may be able to help these pupils find a place in the group. Special skills or assets of the isolated may be used to place them advantageously in groups where their social position can be enhanced.

Jennings has noted that when teachers do not have access to sociometric information, they are unaware of relationships within the group and may even interfere with the development of effective social relationships.

A more adequate picture of the total group enables the teacher to use choices within the group to develop group morale. When one attempts to break up social relationships at random, much of the group harmony may be destroyed.

The child's position within the group is of real significance to his capacity to function. When he does not belong, the inferiority feelings which are created tend to restrict the development of the child's social interest and desire to cooperate. Teachers who use group relationships effectively not only assist the children's development but provide more effective conditions for the accomplishment of their own objectives.

Although it may appear to be easy to size up relationships within the group, research does not tend to substantiate this conclusion. Gronlund[3] found that teachers overjudge the sociometric status and acceptance of children whom they prefer and underestimate the less preferred children. Thus, although some individuals may be more sensitive to a group almost automatically, we should not assume that this is an inherent ability. Teachers will find that sociometric data gives them the type of information which they need to organize the group.

Group Integration

The success of the teacher is largely dependent upon her ability to unite the class in the direction of a common objective. The ability to develop group cohesiveness often determines the learning atmosphere of the entire group. When the pupils are directed toward a common purpose and have established mutual needs, concerns, and interests, learning can proceed without certain kinds of interruptions. This, then, depends upon the teacher's recognition that a group spirit and a group personality exist. She cannot focus only on the most talented or the most disturbing but instead must see the relationships that are going on among all the children. This necessitates overcoming the tendency to form antagonistic subgroups within the classroom. Teachers must be careful to avoid accentuating the differences between groups in order to establish some form of support for themselves. This can only create low group morale. Research continually points to the importance of the development of a democratic social atmosphere for effective learning.

The group atmosphere is most important in developing plans and carrying out work. Divergencies within the group tend to disrupt work, confuse discussions, and limit the progress which can be made. McCleary[4] has shown that harmonious groups maintain the group effort much more consistently in the presence of frustrations than do divided groups.

The teacher, then, must focus on the establishment of mutually shared purposes and values. Development of group morale will prevent resistance to the teacher's efforts. Group morale can be enhanced through the development of communication within the

group. Group discussions provide satisfaction for the participants
and permit the achievement of educational objectives while developing social maturity within the children.

The leader must make a conscious effort to promote a cooperative group spirit in contrast with a competitive atmosphere in which
each individual's effort is directed at maintaining his own place.
Pupils should be led to discover the benefits derived from partici-
pating in the group. As they recognize the interdependence within
a group, they will perceive that their personal significance can also
arise from contributions to the group. Contributions to the group
develop a more effective group and also enhance the development of
the individual.

Group integration can also grow out of enlisting members of
the group in the solution of group problems. The development of
mutual responsibility is an important task for the leader.

In many places we can see that the child's disturbing behavior
is a function of fallacious assumptions or a faulty relationship to
the group.

> A very small child in my kindergarten appeared to be com-
> pletely incapable of sitting still. He was a continual nuisance, re-
> acting intensely to every effort to aid or control him. I had tried
> separating him from the group, allowing him to remain, requesting
> him to take part in group activities, and sternly commanding him
> to keep still and stop interrupting.
>
> One day when his usual incessant activity had reached a high
> peak, the child was allowed to pass out doughnuts, a privilege
> hitherto awarded only to children who had done especially well.
> Obviously pleased, he stood quietly giving out doughnuts to the
> youngsters marching past. The effect continued. He was quiet and
> cooperative and took part in group activities.

Comment: This incident illustrates well the need for new methods
in child management. This teacher went through all the wrong approaches almost in catalog fashion. It seems that almost by accident
she hit upon an effective approach. This incident can give courage
to the teacher who feels nothing works. By permitting the child to
assume a new role in the group his behavior was changed. The
group can serve to effect change.

> Billy had never learned to do anything as well as other children,
> and hence he felt insecure with them. At school he attempted to

gain the respect of the class by doing stunts and making silly statements which disrupted the class.

I tried to help Billy gain self-confidence and feel that he was
important to others. I avoided giving him responsibilities which he
could not carry out, made sure that he had classroom tasks to perform at which he could succeed, and praised him for his ability to do
these conscientiously.

This responsibility and encouragement led Billy into helping
others. In the cafeteria he came to the assistance of others who had
food accidents. He showed other boys who worked with him on the
blackboards how to achieve a streakless board.

He was further encouraged by his classmates when they began
to elect him to serve on important pupil committees. The pupil committee representatives allowed him to participate in group decisions
and to make policy. His ideas were taken seriously. He began to be
considered as a student.

Comment: Here the teacher was aware of the reason for Billy's difficulties. She planfully arranged the environment so that he could
succeed. The children responded to Billy's new efforts by giving
him responsibility. His new role within the group changed relationships within the entire class. The development of responsibility in
Billy resulted in the group's awareness of the benefits of mutual responsibility.

In a junior-high chorus of about fifty girls, Ellen had the reputation of being the class clown. She would do anything in order to
amuse the class. Although she had a good behavior record in other
classrooms, the music room, which had a more permissive atmosphere, gave rise to Ellen's clownlike behavior. She had high musical
ability and had given numerous performances in the area. One
Friday the teacher asked if someone would like to perform for the
group. Ellen volunteered. She began to play in a professional manner, but the class began to laugh and would not stop. Ellen quit
playing with the remark that if no one would listen she would not
play. Someone else performed and was well received, although she
did not play as well.

The teacher wanted to help Ellen understand the group's
action; so as the class was walking out he called her over. He asked
if she would like to know why the class had laughed at her performance, as he could see that she was disturbed by it. He told her simply,
"If you are going to act like a clown you must be prepared to be
received as a clown." He had no more disturbances from Ellen.

Comment: It is incumbent upon teachers to recognize opportunities
really to affect student behavior. This teacher had not planned the

group's reaction to Ellen. However, once it occurred, he could use the incident to create insight. The undesired response of the group served to show Ellen the direction she needed to take for acceptance.

Group Discussions

Group discussion is one of the most important techniques the teacher needs to become acquainted with. By means of it problems can be presented as common tasks for the group. It is really a critical skill that all teachers should develop.

Through group discussion the teacher can acquire information about individual children that she might not otherwise have access to. It can certainly reveal the relationships that exist among members of the class. There is probably no better method for arriving at attitudes held both by individuals and the group. The technique of discussion permits the development of self-understanding and can thus assist in facilitating personal growth.

Group discussion should become a regular part of the pupil's learning experiences. It should be planned for and scheduled on a regular basis. Weekly discussions are a minimum requirement for effective group operation. However, many unscheduled situations develop within the classroom which can be handled most effectively through group discussion. Thus, it should be used in whatever situations seem to indicate that it would benefit the group.

One can expect group discussion to reveal problems that exist within the group. From group discussion the teacher can assess the motives of the group and assist them to develop solutions to their problems. When the problems are discussed effectively, mutual understanding can be developed. Group discussion serves to stimulate enthusiasm and develop cohesiveness. Experience indicates that group discussion is often more effective than individual instruction in the changing of behavior. Certainly, group interaction is most important in the formation of attitudes.

The group leader is most effective when the total atmosphere of the classroom is truly democratic. Otherwise, children will sense that this is something which is more of an act than a true expression of feeling about people and their responsibilities for working out their problems. The leader should be receptive to the children's comments whether they are positive or negative. However, it is well that the leader do more than only permit interaction; she should direct the discussion so that causes and solutions are developed. This necessitates considerable spontaneity on the teacher's part and the development of an inner freedom which permits her to accept differences of opinion.

Footnotes

[1] R. Cunningham, *Understanding Group Behavior of Boys and Girls* (New York: Teachers College, Columbia University, 1951).

[2] N. E. Gronlund, *Sociometry in the Classroom* (New York: Harper & Row, Publishers, 1959),

H. Jennings, *Sociometry and Group Relations* (Washington, D.C.: American Council on Education, 1959), and

J. L. Moreno, *Sociometry as a Science of Man* (New York: Beacon House, 1956).

[3] N. E. Gronlund, *The Accuracy of Teachers Judgment Concerning the Sociometric Status of Sixth Grade Pupils* (New York: Beacon House, 1951).

[4] L. E. McCleary, "Restructuring the Interpersonal Relationships of a Junior High School Class," *School Review,* Vol. 64, November, 1956.

nine | *Deterrents to Encouragement*

Few would deny the need for encouragement or would be unwilling, as educators, teachers, or parents, to provide it for their children. But regardless of how they may try, somehow they fail, often without knowing it. Usually they do not realize the tremendous inner obstacles in their makeup and attitudes that prevent them from carrying out their best intentions to encourage. They often do not know how to encourage; yet, when they are informed and clearly perceive how they could encourage a child, they still find it difficult. A guide toward encouragement would fail in its objectives if it did not clearly indicate the serious deterrent forces operating in almost everyone of us when we try to encourage a child.

The Autocratic Tradition

Our methods of dealing with children, as has been pointed out, are based on tradition. And our tradition was autocratic. Every deficiency, every failure was traditionally considered a violation of demands and obligations not to be tolerated by the authorities who established them. Encouragement was only offered to those children who showed their goodwill in trying to overcome natural deficiencies that were due to inexperience or lack of preparation. Those who were dis-

117

couraged and gave up were regarded as unwilling or contrary and hence required punitive action, not encouragement. As a consequence of this tradition we all know well how to find fault, to degrade and retaliate, to humiliate and exhort; but when it comes to encouragement, we are inept and unqualified.

It is the autocratic tradition that prevents even the most liberal and democratic educator from realizing that reward and punishment are outdated, as Herbert Spencer suggested a hundred years ago[1] and many others have done since. Many still believe that we have to exert force to influence children; when they misbehave, we have to "show" them, "teach them a lesson," repeatedly "explain and advise," but at any rate not "let them get by with it," without punishment and retaliation. Many sincerely believe that these methods have educational value, nay, are essential in bringing up children and teaching them.

Our Social Climate

The autocratic need to impose and to punish has largely diminished in a democratic society. However, our autocratic heritage is still evident. We have become free but have not shed the slave mentality of subordinates who need to be kept in line through fear and who use intimidation to keep others in line, particularly our children.

This tendency to degrade and to humiliate has actually become more intense in our democratic society with its competitive strife, pitching man against man—and the closer the relationship, the more deadly the competition. Each one feels threatened by the other. As soon as our prestige or status is threatened, we react almost instantaneously with a tendency to humiliate. As a matter of fact, our general inclination to feel insecure and threatened conditions us to a constant defensiveness. If we can never be sure that we are good enough, we can bolster our own egos by capitalizing on the faults and deficiencies of others. We become intensely interested in and concerned with the shortcomings of others without realizing that this concern is based less on our good intentions and willingness to help than on our desire to feel superior.

Difficult as it may be to believe, this is the prevalent attitude among members of most families who may love each other sincerely and still struggle to maintain their individual dignity and self-respect at the expense of others who are pushed down or at least are viewed critically. It is simply a question of winning or losing. Either you are superior to me, which I cannot tolerate, or I have to show you my superiority. This takes place in the relationship between father and mother, between brothers and sisters, and especially between parents and children. Naturally, each one will try to gain a semblance of superiority through some accomplishments, through some virtue or ability. But whenever the way to excellence and superiority of achievement is blocked, one does not hesitate to switch to the "useless side" and gain status, power, and superiority through defiance and failure.

The situation between the teacher and her pupils is often similar. As long as the teacher can maintain a cooperative attitude in her students, the contest for superiority and for power does not emerge. However, there are few teachers who do not have at least a small part of their class defying them, and many teachers wind up with more than half of their classes challenging their superiority, their power, and their right to control. Teachers and students often look down upon each other, opposing each other and retaliating with whatever means are at their disposal. The war between the generations penetrates every family and many classrooms.

Under the circumstances it is no surprise that we are not receptive to the idea of looking kindly at the deficiencies that our children use to defeat us. Few parents and teachers recognize that many deficiencies, faults, and disabilities of their children exist just to be directed against them and have a purpose and a definite antagonistic significance. Yet they clearly feel threatened and, far from being inclined to encourage, feel obliged to subdue. It is this dog-eat-dog society of ours which prevents everyone from considering his fellowman as a brother who needs support and help and which drives man against man in the mad rush for personal superiority, creating animosity and hostility among those who should be closest to each other. How can we encourage if we try to push down? How can we help when we actually are interested in perpetuating the shortcomings of our "opponent" at home and in school?

Courage as Prerequisite

It is obvious that our ability to encourage must be limited if not totally absent whenever our own status is threatened. Consequently, we can only encourage if we are sure of our own value and position, when we are confident of our own ability. The more discouraged we are, the less can we encourage others. This does not apply generally, but to specific areas only. A teacher, discouraged and defeated in life, can well be—and often is—a friend to children and may get along exceedingly well with them. Among them he is sure of his place and sees no need to assert his superiority. Conversely, a capable and successful adult, who for all practical purposes can be regarded as efficient and courageous, may find himself utterly at a loss when dealing with children. They may fail to acknowledge his superiority, deflate his ego, tear him down from his throne—and he in turn may valiantly struggle to salvage his adult superiority by degrading them. In other words, the courage which counts here depends on one's self-evaluation in dealing with children. Unless one is self-confident with them one can neither win nor encourage them. Conversely, pessimism is an absolute deterrent to any effective act of encouragement.

Pessimism

Encouragement means increasing the sense of strength and worth of a child. This can only be done when his strength is recognized—his *actual,* not his potential strength. But recognizing a child's strength and his assets precludes pessimism; a pessimistic educator, convinced of the failure of his efforts, cannot possibly perceive them. Furthermore, he does not expect good results from anything he may do. It is unfortunate that our expectations guide us more than our conscious or unconscious intentions. A pessimist is bound to act in such a way that his pessimistic expectations will be validated; instead of helping the child, he will provoke him to become more recalcitrant and deficient.

The general and widespread pessimism of our adult population is the consequence of their being defeated by their children. In turn, their methods of training children constitute a series of discouraging experiences and their corrective efforts with deficient and maladjusted children usually increase the faults rather than correct them.

This points to one of the most important obstacles to the widespread use of encouragement both in our families and in our schools. Before parents and teachers can exert encouraging influences, they will have to overcome the deep-seated pessimism which they usually display without recognizing it. Clearly one must first become aware of one's pessimism before one can hope to overcome it.

Our tendency to emphasize the child's mistakes, the prevalent mistake-centered attitude of most parents and teachers, precludes any encouraging effect. Too much emphasis is placed on the significance of mistakes, too much effort wasted in preventing and correcting them. Instead, a new orientation is needed where the shortcomings, mistakes, and failures will be accepted in a matter-of-fact way, so that the emphasis can be placed on the strengths of each child. This is not possible when the child's mistakes and deficiencies are viewed either as personal insults or as sure signs of impending doom. In such an atmosphere further discouragement of the child is inevitable and encouragement obviously out of the question.

Confusion with Praise

Unfortunately, even the well-meaning and sincere educator may often fail to convey much needed encouragement if he tries to express his approval through praise. No doubt praise can have an encouraging effect on a child. But it may not, as has been pointed out, if the child maintains his low opinion of his ability and therefore considers the praise as unjustified. Praise may have a discouraging effect in the long run, since the child may depend on it constantly and never be quite sure whether he will merit another expression of special approval—and get it.

Praise has too many of the attributes of reward, and a number of research studies show that the results of reward are unpredictable and often have detrimental aftereffects. However, since praise constitutes the simplest form of encouragement, it should not be discarded altogether. However, relying on it as the only means of encouragement may prove to be a considerable obstacle to real encouragement which should increase the self-confidence of the child. It has been pointed out that approval by the group is much more potent. Consequently, neglecting the group, failing to utilize the encouraging potential of the group, is another and very frequent obstacle to effective encouragement. The individual praise given to one child may actually increase the antagonism of his peers and thereby counteract whatever good effect the praise may have had.

Insincerity

Really deep encouragement depends not on a set of actions, although proper actions are important and can be learned, but on a quality which is particularly appreciated by children and which is unfortunately so often missing in parents and teachers. The child feels unerringly whether we really believe in him or merely pretend, whether we give him a pat on the shoulder because we think that is the right thing to do or because we feel with him, with his discouragement and despair, and sincerely want to help him out of it.

There is much talk today about the proper "feeling tone" on the part of adults. We speak about love and affection. They are not always called for or possible, and—even if present—by no means guarantee an encouraging influence. The sincere desire to help, less an emotion than an expression of intent, is the crucial basis for encouragement. Peculiarly enough, children will gladly accept a harsh and even explosive act if they sense the sincere desire to help behind an openly expressed anger. We are too much preoccupied with formalism, with propriety, with good manners, and we forget the deep need for humaneness. As a matter of fact, we cannot even dare to be what we are, to be really sincere in what we are doing, to shed all pretenses of good intentions, because we are so afraid that we may do harm to the child.

The distinction between disruptive hostility and constructive display of emotion lies in the purposes they serve. When the adult tries to salvage his own prestige, it makes little difference whether his attempts to get even with the child for acts of defiance, are expressed in well-controlled coldness, in sarcasm and ridicule, or in outright temper and emotional outburst. The outburst is not the damaging act; its purpose is. An educator who sincerely tries to help a child and blows his top when the child disbelieves his intention, may, by the very display of his hurt and anger, convince the child about the sincerity of his feeling for him. For this reason, we often find an almost unbelievable beneficial response from children to acts of deep emotional upheaval in the educator; children and adults alike can often accept sharp words, which normally would offend, if they indicate a sincere concern and desire to help.

In the rush toward achieving educational goals and improving immediate performance, the educator often neglects the human being with whom he is dealing and merely exerts pressure or even uses bribes for his own ends. Our homes and classrooms are filled with acts of scheming in which the children usually far outmaneuver the adults. Instead of sitting down together and facing the problem, talking with one another about one's real thoughts and feelings, instead of this deeply human form of interrelatedness, we find an atmosphere of pretense, of "good intentions" which actually are not so good and are often expressed only in guilt feelings.

By contrast, in a relationship of frankness and sincerity, whatever goes on has an element of encouragement because the educator and the children face the issues as equals, think about what can be done, appreciate one another in a companionship in which good and bad, superior and inferior, success and failure, lose their significance and their sting. The greatest obstacle to true and lasting encouragement is the unpreparedness of teachers and parents to sit down with their children as equals and discuss openly and freely their mutual problems, their mutual difficulties, and their mutual antagonisms and disappointments. When this is done, the child can grow to perceive his own capacity, recognize his own influence on others, and accept his own responsibility. Achieving this is the deepest form of encouragement for both the child and the adult.

Overcoming the Obstacles

It is evident that cultural factors, traditional concepts, and individual inclinations make the full use of encouragement in our educational practices improbable if not impossible. Instead of indulging in guilt feelings for our shortcomings, we must recognize the handicaps from which we all are suffering in trying to discharge our educational responsibility to our children. Some will find it easy to encourage, and others will have to admit their difficulty and failure; it is important that they be willing to face reality and not indulge in wishful thinking about their own ability and particularly their own good intentions. (By the way, people would be more aware of their real intentions if they knew the function of guilt feelings. Guilt feelings, as we understand them, are the expression of good intentions which we do *not* have. Therefore, we have every reason to be suspicious of our real intentions when we experience the sting of guilt feelings.)

The widespread use of encouragement is, therefore, a goal toward which we all must strive, but which now is only partially obtainable by most of us. Instead of being discouraged by that fact, particularly by witnessing our own failure to provide encouragement, it would be wiser to accept this inevitable consequence of our cultural handicap. The *courage to be imperfect* is a prerequisite for growth; if we try to do more than we can and are unwilling to accept graciously our failures and shortcomings, pessimism and demoralization become inevitable. But if we are satisfied with each bit of improvement, if we can enjoy even a little progress, then we can grow and gain more. Instead of blindly assuming that we *do* encourage our children—which is often a myth—we can begin to see how far from real encouragement our corrective measures are. Once we begin to see that, we can open a door to new experiences, for us and our wards. This would bring a change in our total educational atmosphere.

This brings us to the crucial point. We are part of a general cultural and educational atmosphere, but we are not obliged to continue as victims. In our own changing attitude we do more than become better parents and teachers. In improving our techniques, we change society around us. In this sense, each one of us stands at the frontier of a new society, breaking the ground for new relationships between adults and children. In other words, increasing our ability to exert encouraging influences on our children will enable us to help them, to correct their shortcomings, to improve their growth and function. But in doing so, we do much more; we change the whole atmosphere of the classroom so that learning may become desirable and pleasurable. Therefore, working on our own development is the greatest contribution we can make to our time, to our whole society.

We, as educators, as parents, and as teachers, are in charge of the greatest treasure society possesses, the next generation. The urgent question which confronts us today is whether we will be able to guide them into becoming capable and responsible human beings or whether we will have to wait until youth itself claims its right to proper guidance and education. This question will be decided, in our opinion, by our ability to change from a punitive, retaliatory, and mistake-centered educational practice to one of encouragement for all those who have failed to find their way toward fulfillment.

Footnote

[1] Herbert Spencer, *Education*, Paris 1861.

ten

Analysis of Examples

The intricate nature of encouragement becomes evident when teachers present incidents for analysis. There is hardly a teacher who would not fully agree with the need for frequent encouragement and who would not sincerely try to provide it for her pupils. When all are asked to present examples of incidents in which they acted encouragingly, the difficulty becomes apparent. Many teachers who try to encourage their students cannot report successful incidents. Few examples which are reported demonstrate real encouragement; most appear at best as benevolent efforts.

In this chapter we will present some examples provided by students in our courses. A few are excellent, most just to the point, while some miss it altogether. The difficulty in providing much needed encouragement is one of the reasons we suggest that regular training in encouragement be included in teacher-training curricula. Each student should submit a series of examples to be carefully scrutinized by the class. By the time everyone's examples are thoroughly studied, each student will be more aware of the potential of encouragement and will have a clearer idea of what to do.

The sequence of our examples first illustrates poor specimens and gradually progresses to examples of

127

more effective encouragement. The reader will have an opportunity
to evaluate the reported procedure in the last six examples, which
will not be discussed and analyzed. These will include poor as well
as good examples.

The significance of some incidents presented here is very clear.
Some examples are rather primitive, reflecting simple ways of encouragement, while others are more sophisticated, requiring recognition of their intricacies. Many will give the reader a different impression from the one expressed in our comments. Our purpose was
to point to considerations that are significant and instructive. In
these cases it is not important that our evaluation be the only possible one. What is important is that the examples stimulate the
reader to think and to probe the potential of encouragement and to
become aware of possible pitfalls.

Example 1

Gwen came into my office about one month after school had begun. She was unhappy and dissatisfied with school. In our discussion
I found that she had been highest in her class in elementary school.
Now she ranked only in the middle of her junior-high-school-class and
felt there was no need to try.

I helped her to understand that competition was now stiffer. She
was meeting the best students from many schools, whereas before she
had only her own group to compete with. We discussed the value of
being the "middle" of many who were exceptional, as opposed to
being the "best" of a few.

Through our discussion I feel I encouraged her to work and feel
proud of her so-called "middle achievement," rather than to give up
and accomplish nothing.

Comment: A peculiar form of encouragement. The teacher tried to
convince the child to be proud even if there was nothing to be proud
about, instead of trying to eliminate altogether the need to be proud.
She wanted to convince the girl to be satisfied with her position.
But adopting a new kind of pride will not better the situation. One
can seriously doubt whether these discussions helped in the girl's
adjustment.

Example 2

Most football coaches today agree that defense is 70 per cent of
the game. However, most coaches give their teams the impression that

the offensive team comes first and the defensive team second. This is especially true in reports to the press.

Our team was able to win its first two games only because of its defensive superiority over its opponents; yet the press gave all the credit to the offensive team. After that, the defensive team became much less effective, and we were lucky to get a tie in the next game. I was able to influence the press to give more space to our defensive game and to publish the tackle and assist statistics. As a result our defensive team improved considerably, and we lost only one game during the whole season.

Comment: This is a good example of the difficulty in recognizing encouragement in its essential aspects and the importance of not attributing all improvement to the process of encouragement. Colloquially, one may say that the defensive team was encouraged by the press notice. But was that really encouragement? True, the defense became more effective and contributed greatly to the team's success. But at what expense?

The coach lost an excellent opportunity to teach the members of his team proper values, a team spirit. As a matter of fact, he fortified mistaken values and thereby made the members of his teams more vulnerable for the rest of their lives. He did not realize the obvious fallacy in his position; i.e., that a member of the team is willing to give his best only if he gets personal glory for it. It would have been much more encouraging for each member of his team if he had used the resentment of the defense to discuss the meaning of sportsmanship, the willingness to do one's best even if one does not always get recognition and praise for it. As it was, he played right into the hands of those who consider personal glory as the only motivation for contributing one's best. Providing special recognition in the press for the defensive players did not in any way increase their self-confidence and sense of value; it only satisfied their vanity. Therefore, no encouragement was involved whatsoever. The example shows clearly the important distinction between encouragement and praise.

Example 3

Douglas was six and a half years old when he was put back into kindergarten from first grade because he was unable to do first-grade work. When he entered the kindergarten class, he came through the door hitting anyone in his way. He announced immediately that he would not play with any "kindergarten babies." The boys in the class didn't quite understand and tried to play with him. He was much bigger and stronger than they, and I did not quite know what to do with him. I finally solved this by making Douglas the "teacher" for outside play. He was very good at playing marbles and jumping rope, two things most of the other boys in the class could not do. I asked him if he would help the others learn these two things so that we could show the first graders how good the "kindergarten babies" really were. Douglas immediately became very cooperative and made a wonderful teacher. He was very patient and understanding of the other boys and beamed from ear to ear when he showed them off in front of the first grade. From that time on I had no trouble with him at playtime.

Comment: The teacher used the boy's desire to feel superior and to show off by channeling it into useful activities. She does not say whether Douglas could also function without being on top and without showing off. This would be the true sign of real encouragement. One wonders whether she realized this, since she was proud when Douglas "showed off" his wards and apparently encouraged him to do so. She certainly managed the situation at the playground, but did he cooperate with her during the other hours? He may have done so, although she only reports about improvement at the playground. It is evident that more care is needed to ensure that an apparently effective measure is real encouragement.

Example 4

Joe is an eighth-grade boy, very big for his age but fairly well proportioned for his height. The boys often teased him and ridiculed him about his size. At noon recess he never played with boys of his own age but only with fifth- and sixth-grade boys whom he could rule and who would look up to him.

When I started intramurals with the seventh- and eighth-grade boys during noon hour, I asked Joe if he would be responsible for the equipment, see that it was there and ready for the game. I also asked him to be one of the umpires. He took on this responsibility and carried it out well. The teasing from the older boys stopped, and Joe was no longer interested in playing with the younger boys.

Comment: The teacher succeeded in giving this boy status among his peers. However, one may question both her goals and the effects of her efforts. She surely helped him to get adjusted among his peers, but she succeeded in that by emphasizing Joe's mistaken assumption that he could have a place only when he was special. One may question the teacher's assumption that the boys teased him merely because of his size. It could well be that his size added to his conviction that he was more important. And it was probably this air of superiority which made his peers resentful of him and made him choose younger boys to lord over. The teacher did not counteract this tendency but rather utilized Joe's mistaken goal. Although she helped him to get adjusted to his peers, one may well question the long-range results. Instead of helping Joe to recognize his mistaken goal, she fortified it. In this way she probably made him more vulnerable, because there is no way that one can always be superior.

Example 5

Ervin came to my sophomore English class from the state reform school for boys. He had been sent there for hitting a teacher in the head with a bottle of ink and for stealing money. Not only did he completely ignore everything I said and refuse to do the assignments, but he started in from the first day being a class nuisance. He was deliberately tardy; he brought *MAD* magazine to school about twice a week; on one occasion he lit up a pipe; he brought pictures of nude women to show to other boys; he gave an off-color report on Jezebel when he had been assigned Moses in a "Bible-as-Literature" unit.

My reactions were twofold. Whenever I became completely outraged, I sent him to the office. During the times when I tried to help him, I used what I thought would be encouraging methods. I called him in after school to discuss what he would be interested in doing; I called on him in class to show my confidence in him; I had him run errands for me on occasion. Nothing seemed to work, and he continued his misbehavior. What was even more discouraging for me was the fact that the administration refused to do much about the situation. What was horrible in my eyes was considered not so bad for Ervin. They were working with the juvenile authorities, and I learned that he wasn't going to be expelled and that he wasn't going to be transferred from my class.

Finally, I made up my mind that with any job go a few real headaches. When we started the Shakespeare unit, therefore, I decided I had him for better or worse and I'd just put up with him. No more office calls, no more scolding him; he could do as he pleased as long as he didn't harm the students, the building, or me! About this same time he started something different—writing obscenities on his desk. In line with my new policy, I didn't say a word to him, and I didn't ask him to wash or erase them. *I* spent five or ten minutes after school each night washing his desk. His locker was outside my door, and I am sure that he saw me on several occasions washing his desk.

This continued for about a week. Then one day he came up to my desk and said he liked Shakespeare, and for the first time in his life he wanted to do something. He turned in a Shakespeare notebook and read enough of the play to get a D. The writing on the desk stopped, and his classroom behavior improved tremendously. I continued to treat him in the new way, and I certainly didn't praise him or assume that he was doing any more than he should have been doing. In that nine-week period he earned a D grade and might have passed the semester had he not been returned to the boys' school for parole violation.

Comment: What the teacher did was certainly effective—but was it encouragement? She did two things—she stopped discouraging him further, and she deprived him of his success in defying authorities. The boy found out that there was no benefit in writing obscenities on the desk when nobody took notice. And her willingness to clean his desk was definitely a sign of friendship—she did some work for him. And he in turn was willing to cooperate with her. The essential part in her successful corrective efforts was the change in relationship. Instead of continuing to be a retaliatory authority she became a friend. When she decided to accept him as he was, progress began.

Example 6

Bill was ordered into my world geography class by the principal although it is an elective subject. He had a long history of delinquency, poor school work, and poor attendance. In fact, he was taking only special courses since he was very deficient in reading, writing, and comprehension. On the first day, it was evident that he was indignant and rebellious about having to take this class. I knew it would be useless to try to talk sense to him as that was all he had heard for the last nine years of school. It was also evident that he had run most of his teachers ragged by clowning, wisecracking, etc. So I just ignored him. I put him in the back row so that none of the other students could watch him easily. His reading ability was so far below the class work that I was forced to accept different goals for his work. In fact, he neither finished any work nor even attempted any. About the third week, I assigned oral reports. Of course, Bill was not interested. But when he realized that each student got a library period to work on the report, he asked for an assignment. I gave him the same kind of assignment as the rest of the class received but never even hoped for any results. As the students gave the reports, Bill participated in the class discussion; when I called on him, he got up and gave his report. This was probably the first time he had completed an assignment for a long time. After that, he never missed a class and handed in all the work, and although the quality was low, I gave him a passing grade. It would appear that he was always in a power conflict with all of his teachers. When he found out that I would not fight with him and accepted his work, he became encouraged to be a regular member of the class.

Comment: The teacher is right. Bill's ability to find his place in the class through disturbing and through defeating the teacher did not get him any results in *this* class and with *this* teacher. And his lack of participation in the studies did not get him any results either, since the teacher did not press him to work. Deprived of his usual satisfaction through disturbance and refusal to work, he had to seek new ways to find a place for himself. One can well assume that Bill sized up the situation correctly and tried again in this instance to act contrary to the teacher's demands and expectations—only this time, he could not do so with unacceptable behavior, and, therefore, switched to acceptable behavior. It was a novel way in which the teacher could defeat the student and the student defeat the teacher. And since the old way had been one of mutual discouragement, they *now* encouraged each other.

This example shows how encouraging it is for a student if the the teacher merely desists from the discouraging practices of his predecessors. This teacher did not scold, threaten, and preach as all the others had probably done, and the boy appreciated this lack of pressure and retaliation. However, the teacher probably acted more positively than even he may have realized. One can assume that a teacher who was able to resist being provoked by Bill must also have made some little remarks here and there which showed a friendly attitude and interest in the boy. Otherwise, he probably would not have come around so easily.

Example 7

Just before school was out one evening in the middle of the term, a rather unkempt-looking boy sort of slithered into my room—I am remedial reading teacher in an elementary school. He stood a moment looking at me and said nothing. I got up and asked if there was anything I could do or if he would like to sit down. We stood there another moment, and then I went over to sit down in a place with room for other people to sit next to me at the same table. He followed me over and sat down, but with his feet so placed that he could move fast if necessary.

"Could we just talk?" were his first words. I indicated that this was fine with me—but he didn't say a word. I still didn't know just who he was or what the story was. I asked him if he was in Mr. M's eighth grade room—he indicated yes by a nod of his head.

At this point I felt that if I asked him what he wanted to talk about he would have said nothing and left. So I asked if he would help me with some alphabetizing of cards, which I had been doing when he came into my room. Another nod. He got the cards from the desk at my request, and we worked in silence for about fifteen or twenty minutes. Then he told me his name and asked if he could be in my reading class. I told him about the regulations for entrance into my type of class and doubted if he was eligible because his teacher had not mentioned him, nor had he been mentioned to me in the past couple of years. He countered this with, "You have heard of *me,* haven't you?"

Everyone had, so what could I say? I said nothing but did not deny it. Then he asked me what I heard. I told him that Mr. L, the shop teacher, had told me that he made the best mechanical drawing that he had ever seen done by a boy at his grade level. This was true, and I think it was the only true thing I could have mentioned on the positive side. A big smile and a much more relaxed sitting position followed—and he told me that he had trouble with teachers and with his mother and father, but he knew that he didn't read "very good" (if at all), and would I see if he didn't need to be in reading, and that he would try hard not to be a bother.

Needless to say, he came to my class and was quite cooperative, progressing well.

Comment: This is a description of an effective encounter between a teacher and a difficult, discouraged child. She encouraged him through her success in winning his confidence; she refused to treat him as he expected and was used to. Her perceptiveness enabled her to avoid pressure, and her ability to find something positive to mention made him a friend. It is a wonderful example of a teacher's perceptiveness of a child's needs and her ability to establish a good relationship. After that was established, she probably exposed the boy to many encouraging experiences in working with him.

Example 8

Bob, Joe, and Mike were three fifth graders who had been a constant problem in the classroom since the second grade and were sent to me for remedial reading. After two weeks of getting no place, I dropped all attempts at reading. Instead, we began to talk, discussing various incidents about which the boys wanted to talk. After about three weeks, they began to get anxious. Bob finally asked when we would start to read. I replied whenever they wanted to. The next week the boys took the books which had been considered as too difficult for them and began to read to them.

At the end of the year evaluation was made. The boys all showed better than a two-year jump in reading ability. But most surprising was the additional one and a half years' growth in reading for Bob and Mike and one year for Joe over the summer which showed in the testing program at the beginning of school in the fall.

Comment: There can be no doubt that the teacher produced remarkable and perhaps even unexpected results with the boys. But was it encouragement that produced the improvement? It seems that he removed the power conflict in the reading area. He does not say what kinds of problems these boys had caused in their classroom activities. But one can surmise that they showed the teacher their ability to do as they pleased and their defiance of orders and demands. Their reading difficulties appear to have stemmed from their unwillingness to submit to work and study. The reading teacher sensed the futility of "making them" study and read. He extricated himself from the power conflict. As soon as the boys found no advantage in refusing to read, refusal became meaningless to them. Then they tried to make their demands on the teacher. After all, were they not there to learn how to read? Now the situation no longer demanded any prodding on the part of the teacher—the boys acted on their own motivation and suddenly found that what they could not do before was not so difficult any more. Perhaps the removal of the power contest provided the students with a new concept of their reading ability; in this sense, the teacher actually "encouraged" the boys, even without saying one word about reading. The unexpected growth in their reading ability during the summer when there was no reading class indicates that the year with this teacher provided the boys with a new and more adequate concept of their reading ability.

Example 9

Kim was one of four eighth-grade boys in my remedial reading class. He was reading at a low fourth-grade level; his I.Q. was 103. He had two older brothers who were in the "gifted" class. He seemed to have accepted the role of the baby.

When he came to my class he was charming, but not at all interested in learning to read. The other three boys in the class were working on some phase of reading that we had thought might help them to become better readers. Kim asked me what I wanted him to do. I answered whatever he thought would be of the most help to him. He had no ideas on the subject but said he would do what I wanted him to do. So I had him help me make some phrase cards for another group. The phrases were at a level at which he could read most of the words but not all. We talked about how one could play a game with them and what the student playing the game would learn. He asked if I would like some help in developing some other reading games—which I did.

Kim is going into high school this fall reading at a high eighth-grade level, and he seems to enjoy reading.

Comment: Here we have another case where good results were achieved through the teacher's ability to redirect the boy's demand for attention from unacceptable to acceptable behavior. Kim's reluctance to read was a device to keep others busy with him. He wanted help and advice but was not willing to do anything himself. Instead of pressing him into reading, which he did not intend to learn at that stage, the teacher was able to direct the boy's interest toward helping her. He still got her attention and kept her busy, but this time through some useful means, namely cooperating with her on making the cards and turning them into a game. This he enjoyed, and in doing that he "learned" to read without noticing it. His overambition, stemming from his family constellation, then became obvious. He went beyond the help for which the teacher asked him and voluntarily offered some new ideas—all in the line of reading.

The teacher helped the boy to change his ideas about reading, which now became a source of pleasure, and opened the door to the boy's enjoyment of reading. Encouragement lay in switching the boy's desire for attention from a useless manifestation, through deficiency, to a cooperative and useful contribution.

Example 10

I am a school psychologist. A 17-year-old boy came to me with the complaint, among others, that he could not make decisions. Whenever he had to decide something, he always had to ask others and then usually followed the advice of the majority of those whom he had asked. He was firmly convinced that he never made a decision by himself.

I pointed out to him that coming for help was his decision. He replied, "No, my vocational counselor said I needed help."

Then I called several recent incidents to his attention. HE had decided to cut school one day to have his car repaired; HE had decided to spend the money for his gym shoes on something else; HE had decided not to make decisions in order to ask others for help. At this, he grinned—a recognition reflex. He recognized that he made decisions every day—and said so.

This was a turning point. He progressed in his ability to make decisions and to change them.

Comment: This was an effective approach—but was it encouragement? Making him see his intentions gave him both responsibility and opportunity to change them. The encouraging part was perhaps the change in his self-concept. He could no longer maintain that he was "unable" to make a decision. His greater awareness of his strength and ability to direct his actions can be considered as the result of encouragement.

Example 11

Anne, age 14, weighed over two hundred pounds. The other eighth graders called her "fatso," "large bucket," "tubby," etc. Anne was low average in her school work, sloppy, not too clean in attire, and just SAT most of the time.

I was her music teacher and soon found out that she had an excellent voice. By the end of the first month of school, I organized a girl's quartet, Anne and three other good voices who were also popular, attractive eighth-grade girls. Anne evidenced her first enjoyment of anything connected with school and did well. Once or twice I found it "necessary" to be out of the room at rehearsal time and left Anne in charge. She did well coaching the quartet.

The quartet was asked to sing at school assemblies and various clubs around town. Halfway through the year Anne even enjoyed announcing the selections when they sang in public.

By this time the other eighth graders were including Anne in their free-time activities, and there were no more derogatory nicknames. She assumed a new role in her class. She was not only achieving in music; simultaneously, she was neater and cleaner in her appearance and began to make real effort in all her school subjects.

Comment: The encouragement was provided by the teacher's ability to utilize one of the girl's few assets. The teacher had the perception to build on it and thereby encourage Anne where she needed it most—in her social position.

However, there is some danger in relying merely on encouragement when deeper problems press for a more fundamental solution. There is always a danger of fortifying wrong attitudes and convictions even though their utilization may bring outward success. It is quite possible that Anne acted on the assumption that she had to be something special. The psychological significance of her weight may well be supported by her record as a poor and sloppy student. She probably gained considerable attention through her deficiency. The important part which the teacher played was in giving her the opportunity to have her special place through some positive achievement and contribution. One must be careful with overambitious children who have to be something special at all costs. They need to learn that they can have a place without being special and attracting constant attention. Nevertheless, before the perceptive teacher and counselor tries to effect such deeper changes, an act of encouragement may be needed to make the student receptive to any kind of constructive influence.

Example 12

Nancy, age 4, came willingly to the music room on the first day. She sat on the bench and put her fingers in her mouth. Occasionally she would join the other children in singing, but she did not use the rhythm instruments. I offered her an instrument and asked her if she wanted to play. She nodded. The next few days she accepted an instrument but put it on the bench next to her and then put her fingers back in her mouth. However, she was keeping time to the music by tapping her foot.

After several weeks, Nancy's expressions and movements indicated more interest. One day the children's favorite instrument, the drum, came back from being repaired. I held out the drum to Nancy and asked her, "Would you like to see if the drum works now? Joe tried to fix it for us."

Nancy accepted the drum rather reluctantly, reached for the drum sticks, and looked at me. I smiled but made no comment; she smiled too. Then she started to play the drum, slowly at first, but then enthusiastically. When someone else had his turn with the drum, she accepted bells and played them. Next day when an instrument was offered to her, she first hesitated—I just smiled and said nothing—then took the instrument and played. After that, she usually joined the others.

Comment: Nancy was a child who apparently liked to be prodded and who would have become even more passive had the teacher not refrained from exerting pressure. The important point in this example, however, is that effectiveness probably resulted from her ability to size up the proper occasion for drawing Nancy into active participation. It was not enough merely to offer her the drum, which was the favorite instrument of all the children; one can assume that this would not have been sufficient to get the child out of her passive role. The teacher gave Nancy the function of testing the drum; this seems to be of utter importance. However, such a request would appear as an insincere subterfuge if the teacher did not follow with some acknowledgment that the drum was all right. We have no evidence whether the teacher did that or not. Her smiling at the child would not have been sufficient "encouragement."

Example 13

One of the students in my reading clinic was a withdrawn, self-effacing ninth grader who could hardly read second-grade material. He had the mental ability to perform adequately at grade level, but there seemed to be no way to make him want to improve his reading.

I finally asked him to dictate a story to me. I transcribed it and then typed it just as he had dictated it to me. The result was astonishing. From then on he took an interest in reading, using the file of his typed stories that we gradually built up. He seemed to be amazed that something representing his work could have a neat and highly acceptable appearance. He took particular pride in his name, which I typed at the top of his stories, and his reading ability improved constantly.

Comment: Here is an example of encouragement in its essential aspect. The teacher was able to change the boy's concept of books and printed material in general. Until then, it had been one of distaste and inevitable failure and, therefore, had to be avoided as much as possible. Suddenly the written word appeared in a pleasant way, more than that, as a token of his own accomplishment. Instead of being threatened and frustrated by it, he began to enjoy papers and books, first of course his own, and then others. One cannot maintain a distaste for reading books if one discovers how much fun they can be.

Example 14

Don, a beginning sixth-grade student, had been involved in class-room disturbances to such an extent that for most of the past five years he had been expelled from the classroom. When he was placed in my room, the principal explained that if I could keep Donny in the room instead of sending him to the office to sit there, or making him sit in the hall, or having him clean papers off the school grounds, I would have fulfilled my obligation.

The first day in class I discovered that Donny was interested in carpentry. Later the same day, Don and I were putting away supplies and straightening cupboards when we discovered that there was no rack for storing the different sizes of art paper. We discussed various solutions and concluded that he should design and build a special kind of paper holder. We enlisted the cooperation of the industrial arts teacher and set up "Don's shop" in one of the cloakrooms. Need-less to say, "Don's shop" continued throughout the year, and he re-mained under my supervision because his disturbances were never out of control.

Comment: Encouragement means finding the strength of the child and building on it. This the teacher did.

Example 15

I had a left-handed first-grade boy who had great difficulties with writing. It was impossible to read any of Tommy's work. One day I had a bright idea. I told him, "It's too bad you don't have a left-handed teacher, Tommy. She could help you more easily than I be-cause she would know better how to hold your pencil and all." I told him about a left-handed friend of mine who writes beautifully (this is true) and I said, "She probably finds it harder to tell the right-handed kids how to do this." I laughed, and so did Tommy. When-ever he had a nicely shaped letter in his work, I pointed it out and noted that he was improving. I pointed to letters that were on the line or in the right spaces and ignored the others. He did improve a lot. Although his writing was never good, it became entirely readable and reasonably neat.

Comment: This teacher applied the principle of encouragement. One can show a child the distinction between right and wrong by pointing to the right instead of emphasizing the wrong. But she went one step further. She pointed to her own deficiency in un-derstanding the left-handed children and their difficulties. This removed the sting from Tom's "deficiency"; the teacher also counteracted any possible assumption on the part of the boy that left-handedness is a handicap, an assumption that left-handed children very frequently make if they are surrounded by right-handed children. It is amazing how much encouragement is provided by a teacher's frank admission of *her* deficiencies. It removes deficiencies as a source of humiliation.

Example 16

Mary could not actively participate in physical education class because of a serious ailment. Her parents suggested that she drop out of the class and take music instead. When she talked with me about her physical condition, she seemed extremely embarrassed and wanted to apologize for her "disability." She asked, however, if she could just stand in the corner of the gym and watch the activities.

Mary's mother called me and told me how surprised she was that Mary would show any enthusiasm for something in which she could not participate. The mother also wondered what would happen if Mary did stay in the class.

At the next class I gave Mary the responsibility of being secretary for the class. Her duties were to take the roll at the beginning, write absence slips, and help distribute any printed material. The routine was explained to her, and I gave her the opportunity to watch how I did the paper work. She was completely surprised at being accepted as part of the group and voiced her lack of confidence more than once. I paid no attention to her doubts and let her take over her duties.

When Mary made her first mistake with the absence slips, the office girl brought the slip back. Mary immediately brought the slips to me and began to apologize. My only comment was, "Don't just stand there. Do something about it." I smiled at her, she at me, and her prompt action indicated that she was not further discouraged by a little mistake.

Mary's efficiency and friendly manner won the confidence of the class, and she was soon accepted as referee for many of the games. She was later voted in as secretary of the athletic club.

Comment: Here we can fully see the subtleties in the process of encouragement. Is not the teacher making the same mistake here as the previous one made with Joe in Example 4? Are not these two procedures very much alike? They are not. This teacher did not give the girl a superior status to begin with. She made her work for the class. Only later was she chosen to become referee. Furthermore, finding a useful place for a girl who for every practical reason cannot otherwise participate in the class at all is far different from giv-

ing special status to a boy who does not need it in order to participate. This is one of the subtleties that must be recognized.

Even more important, the teacher recognized the girl's difficulty
in accepting the idea of deficiency. This perfectionism was probably
shared with her mother who simply could not understand why the
girl would want to be in a group where she could not really
participate. The real encouragement came not only through partic-
ipating despite her deficiency, but in experiencing mistakes without
being thrown by them. The incident about the mistake in the absence slips was the real turning point, it seems, although this development was precipitated by the teacher's unwillingness to accept
disabilities as an excuse.

Example 17

Hazel, my third-grade pupil, neglected at home and a social out-
cast at school, caused considerable trouble in the classroom and in
the neighborhood stores by taking things that did not belong to her.

One day when the principal called Hazel from the classroom to
account for a puzzling theft, I felt the girl's need for encouragement.
The class also sensed that she was in trouble again. While she was
gone, I turned to the class and told them that things were not the
same for Hazel as they were for them, that they were shown all the
love and care they needed but that Hazel was not. I told them of the
visit to Hazel's home by the visiting teacher when she had found
Hazel alone and standing over an old-fashioned wash tub trying to
wash a schooldress for herself.

Although heretofore the children had ignored her at the playground and had shown only annoyance toward her in the classroom,
I felt moved at this point to appeal for their help.

I said, "Although sometimes I do not like some of her ways, *I
like Hazel,* don't you?" The group's answer was, "Yes." Next, I suggested that perhaps Hazel did not know we liked her, but couldn't we
show her we did?

The class showed considerable interest now and volunteered ways
of helping Hazel. Some planned to be responsible for asking her to
play with them. Others volunteered to help her with her schoolwork.

After a day back in the class, Hazel had the appearance of a
different child. Before, she had seemed like a little waif, timid and
frightened. One could not forget the happiness that shone in her eyes
when she came into the classroom after playtime, hand in hand with
one of her classmates. Hazel caused no more trouble with stealing and
maintained a friendly relationship with her classmates the rest of
the year.

Comment: This is an excellent example of utilizing the group for effective encouragement.

Example 18

Nancy was shoved into my journalism class because there was nothing else she could take during that period. Although she was a senior and married, she had received little if any recognition during her school years. She did not mix well with the other students with the exception of one girl whom she tried to monopolize. She had little enthusiasm for school work or life in general.

For the first week, Nancy did practically nothing since I set no required minimum of work but depended almost completely on the cooperation of the group for our news material. At one point I suggested to the class things they might want to write about. One of the suggestions was on friendship. This caught Nancy's interest, and she came to my desk to ask what she might say about this. I suggested that she read Emerson's Essay on Friendship and look around in the library for other material.

A few days later, Nancy handed in a feature story on friendship, poorly written but with some good thoughts. I complimented her on the depth of the story and read the paper to the class. The group also liked it, and with some changes in grammar and punctuation, it was published in our next paper.

Thereafter, Nancy needed no suggestions but continued to produce scores of stories on all sorts of topics. Some were good and some poor, but it didn't seem to matter. At the end of the year, her writing had improved to the point where she no longer handed her work to me, but directly to the editor of the paper.

At just what point Nancy was encouraged I am not sure; but I tend to believe it was when I complimented her on the depth of her paper that first time.

Comment: It is obvious that the teacher has become quite aware of the intricacies involved in the process of encouragement. A less perceptive teacher may have thought that merely asking Nancy to write on friendship and her taking up the assignment was the turning point. This is clearly not the case. If the teacher had made any reference to the poor writing and grammar, Nancy's discouragement in her abilities and relationships would have continued. The teacher is right; it needed overlooking the mistakes and emphasizing some important strength and achievement which marked the turning point in Nancy's self-concept about her function in school. If she had felt more sure of her place there and among her peers, she might not have been married so early. This experience in the journalism class will probably have more far-reaching effects on her entire life than may be apparent in this short report.

Example 19

Terry, nine years old, moved to our school district in the middle of the term and enrolled in my room of first graders. This was his second year in the first grade and the third school he had attended since he started school. He was very quiet and shy and played by himself. I tried various ways to draw him into group activities without much success. During a science discussion, he volunteered the information that his daddy collected scrap material to sell. The next day, he brought a large rusty magnet to school. The other children were very interested in the magnet and gathered many kinds of materials to try it on. Using Terry's magnet we experimented with iron pilings, brought in a compass and studied the directions, N., S., E., and W. We invited the principal to come in and share our science discoveries.

Terry continued to contribute interesting articles and demonstrations to our science center. He became an active member of the group, and his reading ability improved steadily.

Comment: The important point of this example is the capital which the teacher made out of an incidental occurrence, Terry's bringing a magnet to class. A less perceptive teacher would have let it go by as an episode, but this teacher utilized the incident to its fullest to give the boy a feeling of belonging in the class which he had never had before in all his school experiences. She stimulated his contribution which was the most effective way to make him feel that he belonged. Feeling his worth in the group, his scholastic deficiencies diminished.

Example 20

This is an example of encouragement which I did not give intentionally. In retrospect, I can see that an encouraging act may often become apparent after it has had its effect.

Judy was a quiet little girl of nine. During my first three weeks as student teacher I was barely aware of her. She was in the low reading group and showed no sign of interest in any work. She was listless and uninspired, messy in her personal habits, and even her art work showed little concern.

Since I was concerned and preoccupied with several "noisy" boys in the class, I did not pay much attention to Judy. After my first month, I began planning the day with the boys and girls. I emphasized that the plans belonged to each of us. We wrote them on the blackboard and examined together the suggestions which were offered by members of the class.

After the first week of this system, Judy suggested an interesting activity for our day. I used it as our first activity of the morning, really without doing it purposely to help her. When we returned from recess, I found her back in the room ahead of the other children. She was running her finger along the words of the daily plan list, reading them aloud to herself. These were *her* plans.

The change in Judy in the next few weeks was surprising. She began suggesting ideas and volunteered information in discussions. Her study habits improved. Most surprising to me, she took a great deal of pride in completing her reading book very nicely.

Comment: There is little more to say. However, the teacher did a little more than encourage Judy by choosing the girl's suggestion. It is obvious from her report that she did not fall for the girl's passive provocation and discourage her by pressure and criticism. Therefore, Judy could respond to the first opportunity that came up to be useful and find her place in the group.

Example 21

Having failed the year before, Peter entered my class with a deep sense of discouragement. He disliked reading and was sure he just couldn't learn it. Even though he was given easy work on his level, he made no effort to do it.

One day I picked a story with very simple vocabulary that I knew he understood. I asked him to read this story for me to three slower learning children, as they needed help. I told him I had other work to do and that I was glad he could help me. He looked bewildered but finally went over to the group. He read slowly at first; then, discovering he could do it, he read quite fluently. He rushed over to me and said with enthusiasm, "That was fun. I never did read a story clear through before."

Comment: This example has a number of important aspects. It shows how overambition often leads to deficiency. When reading became a means of achieving status and superiority, Peter began to like it. One can assume that his dislike of reading was due to the fact that he could not excel in it. His exclamation of "fun" was not because he read the story through but because it was fun to have a superior function while reading. This he had never experienced before.

There is another important aspect in this example which should not be overlooked. The teacher did not merely ask Peter to read to three slower children, which by itself gave him a superior position and perhaps a motivation for reading. She wanted to make sure that what Peter did was really important by pretending that he would help *her* who had something else to do. In this way, she made sure that the importance of his job was properly impressed upon him. Without that, his doubt in his ability may have still outweighed his willingness to read to slower children.

Example 22

In a clothing class on garment construction, a girl worked on a dress for herself but felt all along that she "wasn't the type" for sewing. She was a good student in nearly every field of endeavor, but in this class she was on the verge several times of throwing the dress in the trash basket and dropping out of homemaking. Her lowest moment came when she not only did the stitching on the lapel completely unlike the directions but clipped into the corners so that the stitching couldn't be redone. I suggested that turning and pressing it the way she had done it might be interesting to see.

It was a very "different" effect from the intended pattern, but it amused her because it looked like rabbit ears. I suggested that she do the other lapel exactly like that one and then she would have an original design. When she completed the dress she wore it and showed it off to everyone as her "original rabbit-ears lapel design." Later she asked me if it would be possible next year to change deliberately the purchased pattern to include a few ideas of her own.

Comment: The teacher was able to turn an obvious failure into a complete success as far as the student was concerned. This is an intrinsic mark of an encouraging experience. It helped her to realize that one can make a mistake without becoming hopeless and that making a mistake may even be helpful if one goes on to make something out of it instead of crying over spilled milk. The teacher used imagination and courage when she suggested that the effect might be "interesting." She further encouraged the girl by using the words "original design." The teacher was able to spot the opportunity for encouragement in a most discouraging situation. Doing so, she not only enabled the girl to laugh at her mistake but to stimulate her interest in an activity where she felt completely inadequate before.

Example 23

Steven, a fifth grader, often was an irritant during class discussion and especially during room meetings when another child was in charge as president. He was an "objector" who kept the class and the teacher stirred up by interjecting controversial ideas and objecting to plans to which all others agreed.

For the most part, I had made no comment about this because I welcomed original thinking, but it was obvious that something needed to be done. Reflecting about it, I became aware that Steven's ideas were usually pretty sound. For the most part, he had done some thinking before he spoke. His ideas might often have been of value to the group if his argumentative manner of presenting them had not been so irritating.

I took the first opportunity when I was alone with Steven to tell him how good it was to have someone like him in the class. I told him, "You keep us stirred up during class discussion, but you do it intelligently. You bring up things that are important and thought provoking and help us to consider things we might otherwise overlook."

There was an immediate look of surprise and gratitude on his face. From then on, there was a great change in his contribution. Whenever he had some idea he brought it up with pride and often with humor. He seemed to be working *for* the class now and not *against* it. The children began to look to him for leadership in making decisions.

There was a great improvement in his written work also. Up to that time, it had been very carelessly done.

Comment: The teacher did not give her explanation for Steven's irritating behavior. It is not clear whether or not she was aware of his psychological motivations. But she acted as if she knew them. Perhaps she merely had a vague feeling about them. It is obvious that Steven did not believe in being accepted by the others. He expected opposition and did not realize that he provoked it. The teacher gave him unqualified support. One does not know whether her wording was deliberately phrased, but it was most effective. One word she said made all the difference, and it was probably this word which made the deepest impression on Steven and made him look up in surprise. It was the word "but." She said, "You keep us stirred up during class discussion, but. . . ." Most adults make such statements, and most children are used to them; i.e., to find a "but" after a compliment. At this point Steven could well have expected the following: "but you do it in the wrong way; you argue; you irritate." Instead of that this teacher said, "but you do it intelligently." That was dramatic. And it did not fail to make a deep impression on the boy.

A compliment given in order to encourage a child can be turned around by the critical attitude of most educators who usually add a "but" to a compliment. It can be really meaningful when the "but" continues in a positive way.

Example 24

Gwen, age eight, was left-handed, the second child in a family of five. She had not started cursive writing at the beginning of third grade. She was still printing, not too legibly. Her previous teacher said that she was hopeless, not only in writing but in everything she did. She did not play with the other children. In the second grade, she threw a tantrum almost every day.

At the conclusion of our first formal writing period, I took her paper without comment. I didn't know what to say. She looked at me as though she thought I should and would say something. When we had spelling, I couldn't tell where one word began and the next one ended, nor which way was up. I said, "Gwen, could you spell this word for me?" She nodded. "Then I guess you spelled this, too." She continued to spell the whole list correctly. I wrote a big "C" on the paper. We both smiled.

Gwen began to try to write. By midyear her writing was consistently legible. I found her to be a good student, and she learned to play with other children. When she accomplished something she said proudly, "I can, can't I?"

Comment: This example is of utmost significance. Here we see a child who was not only discouraging to her teachers but also was deeply discouraged by them. She had transmitted her own low opinion of herself to them. It took courage for the new teacher not to accept the reputation the child had made for herself.

Being on her guard, she progressed cautiously—and with great efficiency. She waited for the moment when she could exert a positive influence on the child and did nothing before. Even doing nothing had already had a good effect. The child, accustomed to scolding and criticism, was surprised in not finding it. But let us look at the situation which became the turning point in the child's scholastic career. The teacher described the paper which Gwen presented after the spelling test. We can well assume what the vast majority of teachers would do when confronted with such a paper. What else could one do except reject it totally as illegible? Here the teacher showed her creativity by finding something positive in an apparently entirely deficient performance. Instead of reading what the child wrote, which obviously was impossible, she asked the child to spell the words she wrote. Since this was a spelling test, that alone counted, whether the girl knew how to write or not. But how many teachers would take the pains to find out when they are confronted with an illegible paper?

The teacher's ingenuity paid off. Instead of being continuously and increasingly frustrated by her student, she helped her to develop self-confidence. Gwen was not too sure of herself when she had to express her surprise every time she found she could do something. But she was certainly on the way.

Examples Without Analysis

The next group of examples will not be discussed but left to the reader for evaluation.

Example 25

Peter, age five, was convinced that he could never paint as well as his sister Ann, age six; so he would never try painting during activity time in school. However, he always watched with much interest the pouring and distribution of paints to his classmates. One day I asked Peter to help me pour the paints, which he did; I then asked if he would like to try pouring two different colors together in a jar. Peter was delighted to help and very excited with his new color. He wanted to see the new color on paper. One of his classmates standing nearby exclaimed, "Oh, Peter, you made the very prettiest color!"

Peter was amazed and almost to himself asked, "Did I make that?" The other classmates rushed to see and approve Peter's work. Immediately, Peter offered to paint a special picture and has enjoyed painting since.

Example 26

David, after repeating first grade, came to second grade without much confidence in his ability to do his work. Day after day he either handed in unfinished work or failed to hand in any paper at all. If I insisted that he finish, the work would be very carelessly done.

I soon noticed that David liked to be given little jobs to do around the room. One day when I was sure that David could easily finish the assignment in the given time, I asked him if he would see that all finished papers were collected at the end of the work period. David became very careful to finish his work before he collected the work of the other children.

Example 27

Benny, a tall boy of eleven, came to us shortly after the opening of school with a report card indicating placement in the fourth grade. I tried, with little success, to make him feel at ease and successful in his new situation. It seemed that my every effort to show the boy success and acceptance met with failure.

About a month later his folder arrived. In looking at it I saw that his school record was characterized by frequent moves, poor attendance, lack of effort, and stubbornness. He had been retained in the first and third grades. An intelligence test indicated low average ability.

About two weeks later, during arithmetic class, I happened to notice an excellent pencil sketch which he quickly tried to hide. I asked if I might see it, and he hesitantly pulled it out. I commented on the quality of the work, much to his surprise, and walked away. That day at lunch I sat by Benny and brought up the subject of art. After some discussion I mentioned our need for a background screen in our science corner. I asked if he would make one for us. He gladly accepted the job and used some of his playtime in completing the project. I complimented him on the fine job and expected to mention it to the class. This was unnecessary as they immediately recognized the quality of the work. Each group chairman now wanted Benny in his group. With this acceptance came an unexpected rise in the quality of his work.

The improvement was so marked that around midyear I mentioned Benny's success to the principal. The following day he came in to get a firsthand look. He was impressed to the extent that he brought the elementary supervisor out to observe the boy. A week later, with Benny's approval, he was moved to the sixth grade where he made a satisfactory adjustment in much the same way and continued to do work very near his capacity.

Example 28

Barry was a fifteen-year-old ninth grader who entered my math class at the request of another teacher who was so exasperated with his antics in her room of average youngsters that she refused to enter the room if he was in it. (He had an I.Q. of 74 but was socially more mature and a real showoff.) I gave Barry a choice of workbooks, told him to select one in which he could work but in which he found some new things, and went on with the work of the class—which was not too much beyond his level of achievement.

Barry checked his own work and asked for help as he needed it but did not join in class activities until one day when a spelling test on words connected with geometry was being given. At this point Barry asked if he might take the test and to my surprise scored some 80 per cent of the list of thirty terms. I complimented him on this and asked if he would help me by checking on others in the group who were ready to take a preliminary or retest on the unit.

Barry became quite effective in coaching others in spelling and also in recording scores of those who had "passed." Barry's math still leaves much to be desired, but he is no longer a source of disturbance and friction in the classroom. He asks for and acts upon suggestions from classmates who check his work in arithmetic.

Example 29

Our culture's acceptance of so many forms of artistic expression as being beautiful is probably the basis for the art teacher's approach in which the less satisfying parts of a child's work are ignored and something is found to praise in every piece. Art teaching does seem to deserve credit for being universally encouraging.

Last year I was teaching an art class for the community's summer recreation program. In the class was an eleven-year-old boy who, I learned later, was the despair of his school. The first day there was some horseplay, but since that didn't disturb me it soon stopped. I don't know if he had previously shown any interest in art, but there were qualities in his first drawings that I praised, and I asked him to make others for me. He worked diligently and was soon by far the most successful of the group; he finished several paintings with a truly artistic quality. I enjoyed very much having him in my class. Later I learned that in other groups he was a most disruptive influence. I believe his good behavior was due to the relaxed atmosphere in which he was encouraged to be successful.

Example 30

At the beginning of my third year of teaching on the secondary level, the principal handed me a teaching load which included one class in sophomore remedial reading. I didn't know one single thing about it.

The child psychologist came from the board of education, tested the class, and gave me a list of statistics which showed an I.Q. range of 70 to 114 and reading levels from 2.5 to 7.0. She set up a program in which each child followed a code and read the small units marked accordingly. When he had successfully completed twelve units, he could move on to the next code series. This, I learned, meant that he was ready for reading at the next grade level. Senior girls were assigned to mark the units as they were turned in. All units were filed in single-drawer metal filing cabinets which we all came to call "the cans."

The procedure was stifling to pupils and teacher alike; so on Fridays we gave up "canned" learning and I "bootlegged" a little literature by reading short stories to the class and allowing them to discuss the stories.

In November of that year we were notified that the North Central Accrediting Association would visit our school just before the Christmas holidays. The principal told me that I should plan an assembly program for the occasion. It was a rule of the English department that each English class present a forty-minute assembly program at some time during the semester. My four classes in senior English had already done theirs. I decided to let my remedial-reading class make the attempt.

I said to the class, "WE have a problem. We are to put on an assembly program for North Central next month. What shall we do?" Up until this moment remedial classes had not participated in assembly programs. They were "different," and naturally there was constant dissension on this point. I had battled this being "different" with little success.

When I presented the problem to the faculty, I got the answer I expected: "Remedial classes don't have to do an assembly program." It was an "accepted" fact that they COULDN'T. I asked them if they thought I should have one of my senior classes repeat their program. They didn't like this at all. "OK, somebody think of something," I said.

During the week that followed the class discussed and discarded many ideas. Then Bill (I.Q. 83; reading level 4.2) came up with our solution. "Why don't we act out some of the stories you read to us?" he asked. Pandemonium reigned for a few minutes as the class pounced upon the idea with enthusiasm. "Only one thing," I said, "I don't have time to reread those stories to you. You will have to do that for yourselves."

We divided the class into four groups, three to present stories, one to serve as stage crew, lighting technicians, etc. At that point, we closed up the "cans," and I dismissed the senior girls. For three weeks we worked contrary to all the rules governing a class in remedial reading. The child psychologist came to check our progress and found the class reading books used by regular classes. Remedial readers weren't supposed to read O. Henry's delightful *Ransom of Red Chief* or Poe's thrilling *Masque of the Red Death*. I didn't have time to tell them what the words meant, but I did "import" a set of dictionaries they could understand. Two girls at sewing machines, reading pattern directions for costumes; three boys on the floor with hammers, nails, and boards reading scenery directions; one boy experimenting with a spotlight and colored cellophane and reading light directions. The "cans" had a very dusty and unused look.

Having constructed their own dialogue from their readings, the children presented the two previously mentioned stories and Irving's *Legend of Sleepy Hollow* very well indeed.

"May we do book reports like the other kids?" was the first question asked the day after our assembly program. And so they read— short stories, simple essays going into more challenging ones for those who could take it, and finally novels. We found we had to do some work on spelling because there were too many errors in the written reports. We found that we had to take time out to talk about sentences so that they would say what they should say. But . . . we were "doing what the other kids were doing."

A retest by the child psychologist at the end of the semester showed the reading grades to be 4.3 to 11.0. Joey, the lowest and the slowest, had finally made the grade. He turned in a book report on *Sleeping Beauty.* He had turned in a book report "like the other kids."

Eleven of the twenty we started with made the grade in regular classes during their last two years and were graduated. Two finished taking minimum-essentials courses and were graduated. Seven dropped out for reasons I do not know. I became the remedial reading coordinator for the entire school.

EPILOGUE

The reader who has carefully analyzed the various examples will probably notice an increase in his perception of what constitutes encouragement. He may well be more impressed with its difficulty than with his skill, since we all are more inclined to see our own weaknesses than to recognize our own strengths. None of us is conditioned to be a highly effective encourager; therefore, once we become aware of the inadequacy of our encouraging skills, we may first be even more discouraged than we were before. However, it is hoped that this book will not induce frustration since the reader has now before him a very concrete path to follow in increasing his encouraging potential.

One thing is important to remember: despite our best efforts and most sincere desire, we will never be as good as we want to be and never be able to overcome all the obstacles which a discouraged child presents to us. But if we have the courage to be imperfect, then we are bound to improve. And even without becoming perfect, we can become more efficient, more helpful—more encouraging.

Index

Index

A

Ability:
  control factor to encourage, 119-20
  disability case study, 141-2
  encouragement methods, 4, 50, 51-2
  family relationships, 79-80
  praising, 121-2
  use v. possession, 11
Adler, 41
Allport, Gordon, 7, 10
Art:
  case studies, 149, 150, 151
  skill development, 68-9
  success experience, 92
Assets, pupil:
  case studies, 137-8, 140
  developmental level, 96-7
  encouragement technique, 55, 57, 153
  junior high development, 100
  optimistic approach, 120-1
  readiness, 91
  reading improvement, 63
  science skill, 66-7
  social adjustment, 80-2
  social science skills, 67-8
  speech correction, 69
Attitudes:
  ambition, 41-2
  character formation, 26
  courage, 32

Attitudes (*Cont.*)
  criticism, 148
  deterrent forces, 117
  developing, 23, 70-3
  discussion, 114
  faith, 52
  group relations, 78, 79, 92
  life style basis, 25
  noncompetitive atmosphere, 80-2
  observation, 46
  personal-social adjustment, 76-7, 85
  security, 48, 50, 51
Autocratic atmosphere, 72, 117-8

B

Bakwin, H., 49
Behavior:
  attitude development, 70-3
  basic assumptions, 7-18
  case studies, 128-53
  developmental level, 87-101
  discouragement, 3, 36-43
  groups, 104, 106-115
  motivation, 45-55
  personal-social adjustment, 75-86
Belonging:
  attitude development, 71-3
  group, 110-1
  junior high level, 98, 99
  motivating factor, 53

Reading *(Cont.)*
  improving, 61-4
  intermediate grades, 94-5
  materials, interest in, 139
  readiness case, 135
  Winnetka experiment, 48-9
Recognition, pupil:
  art work, 69
  constructive pattern, 92
  encouragement technique, 52-3, 57
  reading improvement, 62
Repression, 17
Rogers, Carl, 25

S

Science skill, 66-7
Seating arrangements, 53
Security, 48, 50, 51 *(see also* Social adjustment)
Self-concept:
  case studies, 137, 143-4
  development, 75-80
  life style basis, 25
  sibling training, 82-4
Self-confidence:
  art work, 69
  case study, 148-9
  group relations, 110-1
  intermediate grades, 92-3
  mathematics, 66
  personal-social adjustment, 75-82
  primary grades, 89-92
  security, 48, 50
  spelling improvement, 64-5
  stimulating, 52, 57, 62, 92
Self-ideal, 25
Self-understanding, 105, 114
Skills, developing, 58-61
Social adjustment:
  attitude development, 71-3
  classroom encouragement, 103-15
  encouragement techniques, 75-86
  groups *(see* Group relations)
  personality development, 8-9, 15-8
Social context of behavior, 8-9, 15-8
Social inferiority, 37-8 *(see also* Inferiority feelings)
Social interest:
  child development, 26-7
  developing, 77

Social interest *(Cont.)*
  encouragement, 50
  group development, 105
  horizontal progress, 80-2
  personality development, 8-9, 17
Social science skill, 67-8
Sociometry:
  classroom use, 109-11
  individual encouragement, 53
Speech, improving, 69
Spelling:
  case studies, 148-9, 150-1
  improving, 64-5
  primary grades, 90
Spencer, Herbert, 118
Staff, school, 84
Strengths *(see* Assets, pupil)

T

Teaching:
  ambition, 41
  attitude development, 4-5, 70-3
  developmental levels, 88, 89-101
  encouragement material, 4
  examples of encouragement, 127-53
  group encouragement, 104, 105-15
  hopelessness of child, 42
  motivation, 45-55
  personal-social adjustment, 76-86
  pessimism, 120-1
  power struggle, 119
  sincerity, 122-3
  skill development, 58-61
  specific fields, 61-9
  subjective outlook, 11
  technique improvement, 124-5
Testing, 10
Therapy, educational:
  reading improvement, 62-4
  social-personal adjustment, 77, 79
  subjectivity, 11
Training, teacher:
  encouragement training, 4, 127
  group relations, 72
  observation, 45-7

V

Valuing child:
  encouragement technique, 50-1, 57